LOVE TALES OF EARLY JAPAN AND OF EARLY SCOTLAND & OTHER POEMS

by
MATTHEW P. McDIARMID

WITH POEMS
by
DOUGLAS L. McDIARMID

KMP

First Published July 1991

ISBN 1 870978 45 5

Keith Murray Publishing
46 Portal Crescent, Tillydrone,
Aberdeen AB2 2SP

Typesetting by Doges Design
Rembrandt's 'Man In Armour'
Reproduced by British Arts Library

Printed by Mackays of Chatham plc

CONTENTS

PREFACE

My son Douglas was born in Aberdeen 2 October 1950 and adopted days later. Two years from then I was promoted to a post in The Queen's University of Belfast. Within months of the family's arrival there was born his brother, Iain. The twelve years of our stay in Ulster were peaceful and happy, and are so remembered in his poem 'Belfast'. Mention of gunmen dates it long after our return to his place of birth. There he chose to study pharmacy which meant that he did not attend the University but Robert Gordon's College.

About the time of qualifying he met, fell in love with and married a trainee nurse. The disapproval of her parents, their failure to attend the wedding, must have taken something from the happiness of both the occasion and their married life. The couple lived in Perth for a time, but the marriage did not work, she left him and there was a divorce to which his feelings could not adjust. Haunted by 'love's remembered hand' - the story of his love and its consequences for him is in the poems - in a state of acute depression, feeling that life had rejected him, at Gravesend 2 January 1980 he took his own life.

Yet unusually tall, active, sociable, he sought and made friends easily, as was attested by the numbers who attended the cremation service in a town where he had not long resided. Naturally kind he liked people, would visit hospitals, loved beauty as he found it in the countryside, supported the anti-nuclear cause, features as evident in some poems as his griefs in others. I knew nothing of his verse till after his death, a loss to poetry. My copy was lost but found by his brother. With peace of mind he would have written more and more happily. His ashes lie beside his mother's in Neilston Cemetery, Renfrewshire.

Concerning my own poems, which form the greater part of this book, I would specially hope that the 'Tales' escape the unconsidered, still lingering, prejudice against poetic narrative. Primarily tales, any poetry they achieve is occasional or resides in the final effect. Indeed it might be better to speak simply of rhythmically heightened story-telling, the impression that action and expressed feeling make being thus intensified and given that further dimension that prose does not normally attempt. The short poems will be judged in the usual way.

Like the form that best expresses it, the love theme that is in all my tales is given comparatively little space in modern verse, yet it is a theme more capable than most of noticing the more general, universal aspects of experience.

Sources for the tales, the kind and degree of their use are in the notes. Only 'The Geisha' adheres to basic events, and even so the treatment is my own. The other tales of Japan select an interesting event and person and develop them originally, thus `Captain Narihira' transforms an incident and gives to its poet- hero imaginary life, loves, poetic history, poems of my own. 'The Go-Between' has for heroine a very minor character in the great classic **The Tale of Genji**. Tales of Scottish origin get the same free treatment. Some of the ballads, like my unifying concept of a 'Land of Balladry', are my inventions, so also Old and New Orpheus'. In the case of 'The Boy', bits and pieces from several tales have suggested the one story. None the less, it must be said, 'without the great early Japanese classics, in Scots the ballads and work of Robert Henryson, nothing'.

For the Japanese tales my debt for suggestions to the instructive mid-nineteenth-century anthology of A.B. Mitford Lord Redesdale and the more comprehensive one of Donald Keene should be clear. To the lady Reiko Aiura of Kyoto, formerly a student of distinction at the University of Aberdeen, I owe useful information and criticism. She is not to be held accountable for the un-Japanese traits of my story-telling. It should help the reader to know in advance that I have chosen to pronounce these names as follows - Tokubei: Tokubay, Kashīwagi: Kasheewagee, Shirai: Sheerāee, Narihira: Nareeheera.

A final statement must be made, that my poems in this book could not have been written without the patience and inspiration of my dear deceased wife, Helen.

MATTHEW P. McDIARMID

This book is dedicated

to the memory

of my wife Helen

POEMS

by

DOUGLAS L. McDIARMID

BELFAST

My city is at peace, is still,
just as I knew it when the gunman's kill
was not the small talk of the street,
when no child saw the soldier keep
the curfew of the night.
Still in my memory, not now, redbrick
it wore its dress of dirt with a clean pride.
Harland and Wolff's outmatched the facing Clyde
for its tall ships.
Each dingy factory and petty store
as a dull day in a bright week
wore borrowed light,
was new, unique,
then to my schoolboy sight.
Centre and windings from it all I knew
and know them yet,
the Lough and lands about it too.
Still in the bushes about Barnett's Park
a small boy plays his game of hide and seek,
goes handed with his father through the dark
to home and storied bed.
There was my school,
there the recorder fingers learned to play
is playing yet
the tunes that do not go away,
as 'Frère Jacques', 'Three Blind Mice',
and high and shrill above them all
'The Londonderry Air'.
If I forget thee, O Jerusalem!
    Yes, childhood was a city called Belfast
and I grew up to wonder where it went,
my town so innocent.
The name may last,
but on what map to seek it, what it meant?
In Ormonde Park, my street, a bell was rung
and the householder answered, was shot down,
with him his watching daughter, a mistake,
they bore another's name.
Such things they say now of my town.
And still the child is playing in that street,
in a young city grown he will not find.
Nor will he try.

As well he left so it could never die
and he remain to run its parks again,
and days as peaceful rainbow in his mind
and no dawn break to prove the bow a lie.

★ ★ ★ ★ ★

CHILD'S PRAYER

God bless my mummy,
Take care of my dad,
please bless my brother,
and I'll be glad.

Keep our house lovely,
inside and outside neat,
don't send the gunman,
at least not in our street.

Why don't you come here
O dear father of all?
What do you look like?
Are you very tall?

I don't know your religion
and don't really care,
just look after us,
and that's my prayer.

★ ★ ★ ★ ★

THE GUNMAN

It came into his hands like God
moving His creature, thunder rolled,
echoes still rolling in his brain,
nerves tensed with power beyond his own,
a hand of glory. Now he knew
the deadly innocence of Cain,
used by the means there at his side
and going pleasured on his way,
mindless, his brother lying still.
Or it was like that other force
that lifted lovers to delight

and their used bodies left inert
and speechless in the ravished night.
Compare it as he would, it was
the liberator of his will,
the mirror that gave back his truth.
Orders would come, why this one man
or that simply he did not care,
he took his orders from the gun.
The target sighted that was that.
No hero of a chosen cause,
a trigger-finger, nothing more,
when had he been responsible
for life or death? He was a hand
for which the gun had frequent use.
    The boys are playing in the yard,
'Bang! Bang!'
One falls at once to rise again
and all go home unhurt for tea.
As some will not, as some will not.

★ ★ ★ ★ ★

HELL

The hunter on the hill,
was it above his kill
when empty eyes looked back
so speakingly
to haunt his dreaming night,
that hell was born?
The forest with its many voices told
how many its tree-folk,
how lasting was its life,
and of their endlessness
the rivers talked,
mountains and steady stars.
Something about his kill,
the creature there so still
spoke the same endlessness.
He knew what dream would find him in the night,
Under the earth where all life went its course
the beast still fled,
the hunter close pursued, and then

it turned on him,
the hunter fled, the beast pursued,
here there would be no kill.
So lively drawn the cave walls of Dordogne,
a hand of knowing fear.
Bison and auroch live
not to give magic power
to throwing arm, hand-thrust,
but in the gusty light
let the tensed hunter see
his heaven and hell
as in the killing day, fled night.
Ember and flame still nursed, still feared,
did the tribe read in those red eyes
and on the glowing walls
the undying beast,
hear the undying hue and cry
through the long caves of night,
the hunted they?

★ ★ ★ ★ ★

With head on hand
I lie and dream
on a far land
past sea and sky,
dream to its tunes
mild sea-winds play,
flowers on the dunes
dance gracefully,
red on the sands.
Why say I dream?
I feel the winds,
I see the flowers,
sands, sea and sky.
It is our gift,
our human gift
in near things far
another land
to see and hear.
Nearest to hand
the best dreams are.

★ ★ ★ ★ ★

Even as it wells
the rippling water seems
eternal, full of life
and lovable,
so mischievous it smiles
up at those adult trees.
'Play now', it hears them say,
'one day there comes the sea',
meaningless word.

* * * * *

So beautiful
the spreading flower.
Round it time slows
to let us look at it,
how fair it grows.
This slowing you will find
happens where beauty is
in any kind -
though where love comes
time also speeds,
resolve that if you can.
One thought is that a flower
will bring you peace,
as love will not.
I look upon the rose,
a head of beauty
lifted to the dawn
in quiet courage, so
its colour shows,
still living on
short as its day may be,
and as it knows.

* * * * *

We do not hear.
Birdsong in summer rain,
though it come near
is lost to listening.
No wings fall to our hand
above the graingold land

or garden flowered.
Men have made birds be shy,
give to the safer sky
their harmony.
And yet they tell of some
gentle, so as they played
their instrument,
to them small birds would come
and them accompany,
a music from us strayed
and to be found again
briefly, and then with pain,

★ ★ ★ ★ ★

KING SOLOMON

In all his glory Solomon
was not arrayed like one of these
lilies that set the fields afire
with beauty, daughters of the wind,
if Christ was right, if Christ was right.
But Solomon
took beauty to his bed at night
and did not walk the fields to ease
his world-sad eyes. Unquiet fool
he sent across the sands for silks,
cedars from Lebanon made yet
more great his house, but for his god
with stone a needless temple built.
Where now the prophets' Israel,
the rule of men who only heard
their god, and heard him everywhere?
Palaced, guarded by men of blood
long corridors he walked with guilt,
his judgments were recorded by
scribes who must take their stint of bread
low at his tables, nothing said
of taxes that made poor the land
and good men that denied them die.
Of course, the great king must be wise.
Not his 'The Song of Solomon',
the play of the sad Shulamite,

though voices from it cried to him
as if his own, lips on the lute
complained to night and wept the dawn.
What then in fine of Solomon?
A folktale king, and Christ could smile
counting his glory foolishness
beside the meaning of a flower,
and Christ was right, yes Christ was right.

* * * * *

Child of the night,
a moment there unhelmeted
I saw your painted face, dead-white
beneath black brilliant hair,
and you were gone,
your angry byke's companion roar
defiant of the dismal street,
spearing the dark with speeding light,
darkness made darker than before,
and on
where house and hedgerow from you flee.
Does the dark make such difference
to your day self, and is that self
so other made
and lifted by the power you feel
charge that slight body as you race,
the nightwind lashing at your face,
wild earth, wild heavens felt to reel
past in as headlong pace?
In black and white as on you speed
what is your so compelling need?
Is it youth's unavailing rage
as yet unconscious of its aim,
against that slow but certain step
heard coming down the way of years,
the step of life-accepting age,
or just adventure, the unknown
dark land you face and face alone?
What are you when the night returns
you quiet to that dismal street,
your all too ordinary kin
and comfort of your naked bed,
and morning sends you frocked to work

by tube or bus? Machine uncharged,
young witch with broomstick laid aside
and waiting with the moon to ride
in covine full,
or just another girl unwed
with thoughts of children, marriage-bed,
or none of these,
darkness still find you on the road,
child of the night?

★ ★ ★ ★ ★

A hand goes up
above the crowd,
a cry of pain,
a cry so loud,
yet no one heeds,
a cry in vain.

The crowd runs on,
'Must catch the bus!'
and does not stop.
'What's all the fuss?'
At five o'clock
the town goes pop.

★ ★ ★ ★ ★

The high hid path, it runs through hills
in green tranquillity,
the birds into the sun they sing
out of eternity.
Are the lands real the path runs through?
No one that takes it knows,
but still they find the secret road
and light on it that glows.
Islanded on its sunshine path,
high over summer's sea
I stand and guess at pebbled sands
and children running free,
I guess at beauty, something more
than suns or summers send,
a light along the secret road
only with dreams can end.

★ ★ ★ ★ ★

Yes there were moments when the sunshine burst
out of that ancient book, a brighter dust
than calfskin board or yellowing leaf could yield,
moments when man felt new and free to dream.
Of course, they'd found the golden-lettered word
PEACE and the promise of a golden age,
found it with time to learn what it must mean
to discontent that is an inborn thing,
how the bright promise palls, best days the same
make restless minds look evermore for change,
the too soon angry spirits that men are
make much of difference, country's or faith's,
revive old loyalties, live hates anew.
I write amid the ruins of a war.
So a wise man would wish the book shut fast,
no burst of sunshine to make dance the air,
but the due round of days, men at their work
with no thought past it save what touched their loves.

★ ★ ★ ★ ★

NUCLEAR EPITAPH

'The evil place Death brought me to
is not the one in which I lie,
but that were at a single touch
I made a race and planet die.'
We who are from Arcturus graved
these words for one good soldier's tomb,
Death that should need such little space
took all a world to be its room.

★ ★ ★ ★ ★

Joe ploughed his fields,
farmed well his land,
and Joan gave birth,
gave him a son.
The air was clear
the day before,
neither would ever
understand.

★ ★ ★ ★ ★

The weeds can see
we're talking now
and fighting now,
they bow their heads
in thought for us.
Remember them.

★★★★★

Steal as it may its life from hidden root
grown from the seed left by the eddying air,
triumphant shows upon its stalk of green
the final flower, there with the wind to share
beauty. So with such secret strife
swaying yet seeming still,
for in perfection always stillness seen,
sunward the rose will climb with earnest will,
life will be its. And yet,
why do I stand and look
at what the wind forsook
and chance let grow beside a country lane?
Not for its beauty braving tallest weeds,
no, that so red, red stain
speaks to an ancient pain
and new, now gladly mine.

★★★★★

We came in Disco Land
and saw the coloured crowd
move to the latest sound,
swaying like trees.
Silence would crash, a while
couples stand still and smile,
waiting to sway again,
movement was language.
Light strobed the throbbing air,
bodies were all we were,
the dance was danced elsewhere,
until the last sound fell
on Disco Land.
We came away,
out on the quiet square

our bloods still throbbed, still pulsed,
their answered question.

★ ★ ★ ★ ★

There was a call,
and for the highest stakes
a man, his woman, at the table sets,
a choice that courage takes.
An error, chance could deal us saddest debts,
the heavens could fall.
Yet I said, "Let's,
Time the great croupier rakes all in,
'Monsieurs, mesdames',
his call may see us briefly win.
We place our bets."
The wheel was spun,
where it would stop we did not care,
life could begin.

★ ★ ★ ★ ★

In bliss of love, you lovers say,
have you stayed long?
I think not, whence comes all its force
of sweetness but from transience?
A passing thing the aeons found
a flower must be, no less a love
or life itself.
Creation knows no other way
to give perfection to that state
we men call bliss in love.
As morning showed me when you woke
and smiled
for last night's dear remembrances.
A thousand ordinary days
without regret I could have lost,
bent there above you, just to see
in the mere moment of your smile
all that it meant.
You lovers know well what I mean
when I say all my asking is
transience eternised in bliss.

★ ★ ★ ★ ★

Moonlight itself a sea
flowed on the waters,
flowed on the quiet sands
where slow we wandered
and with few words between,
where with the touch of hands
a tide so vast came in
and gently took us.
Up on the darkening dunes
swayed the tall grasses.
Stars from a summer sky
stared on a world at ease,
and easeful lovers. That
white line, where sea on sand
fell and came into die
again and yet again,
told us just so to seek
what life now gave us.
Far out a questing gull
uttered its lonely cry
unanswered and was gone.
Questing we too had been
but answer there had come,
and on our moonlit walk
handed our loves went on.
Happiness so extreme
more than itself must mean,
more than where we had been,
somewhere the whole world went.
Only a moment, but
it had an endlessness.
So the night let us dream
as the bright wave came in
upon the sands unspent.

★ ★ ★ ★ ★

'We'll watch how green things grow,
how new lives come and old lives go,
we'll not leave out the smallest thing
that life should know,
and age that trails a broken wing
still it will sing'.
    Is this not folly, make such vow

when time will move as it does now,
all scenes by hope pre-set may change,
make our young loves seem quaint and strange,
bring to our eyes the bitter tear
for loss of what was held most dear?
No, it is faith, and what we mean,
open, apert and public seen,
we let the world know with a ring,
and if this still is not enough
we call to witness our true love.

★ ★ ★ ★ ★

I had a dream and the dream strangely true,
in which the skies released a jewelled shower.
Mine were the skies, their rubies, emeralds,
and as they came the whole it changed and flowered
and sang in thrilling voice to its flower sun
that, as dreams will, was suddenly grown you.
And yet not day, my night skies did not spare.
I woke, we lay as the first dawn quite bare
to all the gifts the heavens had to give
their first of men. Given, to give again,
was the most precious man and woman know,
that you receiving gave, I gave and won.
Such dear exchange of presents lovers make.

★ ★ ★ ★ ★

What but a passing beauty should
window eternity,
as one day dawning in your eyes
something you let me see,
something that had a lastingness
so the years lost to love,
if that could be,
remembering that moment might
think that it was enough.

★ ★ ★ ★ ★

The planet's revolution on a dial,
the natural procession of our sky
shown here in the slow change from light to dark,

once told the small divisions of our day
in gentle way,
time did not fly,
it kept an easy if a certain pace.
I like to think men then felt free,
against the hour no need to race.
New time is not the same,
we are its prisoners without release,
its strict conditions age or death must mend,
for now we look to metronomic hands
to point precise the terms of work and play,
even the racing seconds we must mark,
men are machines or seem to strive to be,
the dial no longer points us, it commands.
And yet we find a way to make time cease,
one where no thought comes, yet makes to its aim,
desire has its own purpose and for end
achievement of a stillness and a peace.

★ ★ ★ ★ ★

We sailed the sea now grown so calm,
late turned so wild, and still alive
so good to be sea-worthy thought
and clasped our hands, for wrecks about
told what great waves could come and strive
to break our timbered peace. But now
gladly as carefully we sailed.

★ ★ ★ ★ ★

Now day to night,
inside to out,
odd the world goes
when walked alone,
yet time is found
to set things right
and make for home.
A little flame,
the merest spark
still burns away
the closing dark
and brings the day.
Still we can love,

still put things right,
find home again.

* * * * *

To whistle up a wind, fill my black sail,
so that from this dead calm I could win clear!
But I lack instrument, my ship will stay
and my sail still be black. This though I know
if there should come a clean forgiving rain,
and my too angry self more gentle grow,
my black sail then would fill, its colour change,
and I win free again.

* * * * *

It was as bright a tunnel
as train could enter in,
lights shone, flashed by, the tunnel
was one with the bright train.
Barely we felt its wheeling
along the rails of night
and in our death of feeling
cared little, stop or go.
One way to end the tunnel,
stop the train speeding on,
was to step into darkness
yet deeper than our own,
if any such there were.

* * * * *

She went, he stayed,
and still the record played
to the last word not last,
the anger no space cools
of two embittered fools,
raised voices, late regrets,
for neither hate forgets
so much of beauty lost,
the pain and all the cost.
Just something that life sent
the onetime lovers say
and hear the record play

relentlessly.
Now at the best they live.

★★★★★

A painted tale,
portrait in blue,
dark for the hair,
for the face pale,
someone I knew
who still can move
a memory.
You ask how could
these shades in blue
be given love.
They spoke my mood,
I painted true.
Time does not blur
the features clear,
and when I see
how others fare
as lucklessly
feeling must share
their hate, their love,
their need for her.

★★★★★

COLOUR

Green winked a wicked eye,
brown was more modest,
blue spoke a summer's sky,
autumn was yellow,
red meant a rose, and black
bore up death's banner,
I lived amidst colour.
Once there were fields of it
freshened and flowered by it,
crowded streets loud with it,
corridors of colour!
Now field and street alike
into a sameness run,

windowed and wayside path
nor mind nor meaning show.
Colours so many once
are one that will not go
so that time's hand moves slow
from grey to grey.
Why? Let the lone wind say
that, among flower and folk
goes colourless.

* * * * *

In the beginning was our word,
effected with our deed, with such kind world
of loving, late unmade, rendered absurd
to my still hurt remembering, our good
creation waste and lost, and for that loss
what feeling chaos come! Oh I could bawl
my bruises to deaf heavens, make them hear,
travel to poison the world's well in hope
you drank of it, and loving drink it too;
wish we were damned in hell so that we shared
its ice and heat, as once we shared the sun,
your known guilt gnawing never felt the less,
my hate still fuelled by remembrances
of what you meant, and still must mean to me.
Kindness the day requires, but you unkind
make me forgive neither myself nor you.

* * * * *

Love and you live,
share and you have.
I hope still to be alive
when you
no longer have nor give,
and there
is nothing for which to strive
but my forgetting you,
and this I shall not do.

* * * * *

Do not approach my valley,

my stream and lonely creek
that winds the hillside withered
about the glooming peak
and castle black on it.
Nor come see dead the grass,
the air feel more than still,
note here how no birds sing
and know they never will,
here's neither night nor dawn.
Let the unchallenged gate
guard still the ghastly sight
and the unentered room
keep, in that faded light,
the dim, the lifeless scene,
of fire and furniture
emptied the hall and bare.
Only a woman's skull
holds court upon the floor,
still with black burnished hair
tressed round the eyeless stare.
Trumpet, be still, and you
good knight ride on your way,
no watchman on the tower
will heed your idle bray,
no one, nothing's within,
nothing as from the day
my lady went, and I
walked by the lonely stream
and saw against the sky
both peak and castle black.

★ ★ ★ ★ ★

The boy that lived his myth
remembers as a man,
there was a fireside once
and flames that gently danced,
there he was warm
and love about him went.
So life began.
Later he lost his myth,
fire beyond fireside flared,
the heat of young desire
that burned through restless days

towards no imaged home.
Yet the myth came again,
its joy and peace
briefly, so briefly shared.
Now that fireside is gone,
and yet his world of myth
still in a lonely room
and from an empty grate
speaks of his perfect hour
and home not lost,
empty where flames once shone,
where from a seat beside
came love's remembered hand.

* * * * *

AT BANNOCKBURN

I motored north, I had to break the news,
met father, mother, brother, on the field
of Bannockburn and the remembered day.
Banners were bright and frequent on the air.
It seemed
all the defeated nations were come there
as victors in their loyalties,
and naturally on that ground
the Scots were loudest, fullest in array.
Whole companies were set to celebrate
and to make holiday
for the great victory that kept them Scots.
World wars had come and gone but this meant more.
We strolled about, briefly heard speakers, were
for these few hours again a family
all as in years before.
Our talk touched little things,
what this friend did, what that, the good times shared,
touched on the holidays we'd take
now the good days were come, such trivia
as keep men sane. As if well understood
of one name nothing said.
    It was midsummer and the longest day,
and the delaying sun still shone
on field and Forth, just as when Bruce first saw

the expected pennons come
and surcoats angel-white,
so many that they covered all the ground,
but in our talk and laughter memory
of that well fought, well planned-for fight
was momentary and had little place.
Something I had to say I think they knew,
there was consent that it could wait its time.
Near about five we moved towards our cars
and to the moment when I broke my news,
unhappy as the answering "That's life",
all that there was to say.
Lives two years separate at last the law
this battle had ensured would still be Scots
pronounced apart.
That both could use my name was the least hurt.
And yet a bright forgetful day
is what stays most in mind.
They motored north, I south.

* * * * *

For some the love that has no end,
for me first love and last the same,
my brief, my bright eternity.
Brief as
that point to which the passions tend
now seems our love.
A moment, a mere moment then
I lived an everlasting day,
and the day went.

* * * * *

THE PATH

The way is hard, and then most hard
when some bright moment from the past
shows me in full extent my loss. Then am
I prisoner to past and present both,
so stayed. And always there's the way to find.
I would not but for those brave sounds
so far, so faintly borne.

Somewhere a path is leading me
untried before, where people dance
to tunes of freedom.
Somewhere the light winds know is such a land,
the small leaves know, the wanton wayside flowers
that give themselves to joy and to the sun,
and I may chance upon it as I go
and dance as free.
Not that the past will loose me and unhold,
so fast the grip it lays on memory,
but that I shall not care.
Meanwhile I walk and tunes from far away
tell me my path.

★ ★ ★ ★ ★

THE SIGN

The land was mine, just for the take,
roadless and smokeless, not a sign
someone had been that way before
or ever seen how green it looked.
I entered it, and only then
felt the great loneliness press in
from sky and hill,
fields that had not a farm in them,
not a live house, grass that gave back no sound
to my slow feet.
If in a silence no bird broke
summer its full appearance showed
in bush and tree,
yet time that's seasonal was nowhere felt.
Thus gradually I came to know
the land not mine,
as waiting its true settler with the sign
not mine to give,
the will, the joy, to live.

★ ★ ★ ★ ★

I watch the grasses sway
in shadow dance,
shadow with shadow play

to the sun's glance,
and free I walk my way,
I make new tracks.
Into the sun I fare,
my shining rest,
of all
man's destinations known
this one the best,
nowhere.

* * * * *

The gates of time
that shut me in with birth,
my foolish birth,
and their gatekeeper fear,
they do not keep me here.
A little push,
they open, I walk out.

* * * * *

LOVE TALES OF JAPAN

LOVE STORY[1]

It was in Maytime, month of flowers, he came,
and to Kyoto, where the women are
most skilled in flower arrangement and know best
the ceremony of the tea, as she
had practised them, but that was in her health
before the sickness and the sufferance,
the long, long wait at home preferred, so soon
to cease. They talked of crisis, end or mend,
she knew which it would be. Grace she had loved,
it would be at her end, the few flowers set
to wish, against due colouring. That done
eyes dreamt. Of course, better than doctor he
knew all her case and when to visit her.
    Spring, pleasant Spring, unfailing in its signs,
when every tree bore blossom on the bough
and loveliest the cherry and the plum,
when each park, painted pink against blue skies,
was walked by handed lovers, and desire
was one more growth the season brought to flower,
and the most urgent, it was in this time
Death turned into the street where the girl lay
not long for life. As any other day
he did not hurry, though the sunshine may
have made him loiter just that little bit.
He found the house and mounted the short drive,
reached the locked door, the room where he would play
his part, stood by her bed and looked. It was
as I have said like any other day,
at least for him whose action was the same.
    Yet as his finger almost touched her heart
it stayed, such ordinary reasons yet
it stayed, nothing to set the girl apart,
nothing to make him break his nature's laws,
yet something did and so he stood and stared,
things should have happened elsewhere that did not:
hair of a midnight blue, eyes inwardly
scanning strange heavens worlds and worlds away,
pale, pale, their glance and glistening to white.
Pictures came to a mind sent wandering.
He thought of swans like ghosts on evening's lake
sailing whereto he could not understand,
the busy cygnets plying in their wake,

the swans still sailing, to what end they knew,
of ships white-sailed upon a shoreless sea
with no aim he could guess, unless it were
in that vast loneliness companionship.
He saw her breast still moved, a child should be
at it in shared content. He fell in love,
and as he did the eyes now clear smiled back
and he again. Death no more Death felt life
and shed his ghostly being for a smile.
'You need not be afraid,' it seemed to say,
'you are as any man,' and it was so,
that he was flesh and blood. Another voice
within him said, 'It happens, someone else
will come for her one day and she will go,
and come for you, and then you will have known
both hurt and kindness that are Death's to give.
Meantime you love as other mortals do,
and where love goes, that too is yours to know.
Its days are brief, use them as best you may.'
The voice was silent, would not come again.
The universe was very small, her eyes,
her smile, and it was very simple what
he felt. The swans sailed still their evening lake
but now he knew whereto, why they were paired.
The ships moved still upon a shoreless sea
yet had their aim. Her lips were very near.

Note:

1 This tale has no Japanese or other source, only my fancy.

THE GEISHA[1]

The teahouse on Osaka's front looked out
past lane and land to Sonezaki wood
and river glittering in dancing light,
a scene that owed its colours to the sun.
At that late hour most blinds, not all, were drawn,
lovers slept off their labours of the night,
the house that looked on space and far afield
could scarce have noted the close lane beneath
then unfrequented save for the one man.
With noon a change would come, life fill the lane,
geisha[2] lips red in a white face, teeth blacked,

descend and move among the customers,
wooing with practised smile to the tall stair,
their bedded room. Quiet would reign again
with hot still afternoon, but coming night
would see life louder, more desirous yet,
crowd the establishment. At all these times
the house seemed waiting something where it looked,
to Sonezaki's green and rivered wood.
    Ohatsu heard the step she knew so well,
flew to her window, cried: 'My Tokubei,
where have you been these two long loveless months?
How I have missed you, how these woman's breasts -
she clasped them to her as if tender flesh
best spoke her tender hurt - have ached to feel
your hands on them, the brush of moving lips!
This body left an idle slighted thing
has lain and longed to feel the use of love.
Surely my clients must have felt me fail
of the full gift of self that once I made,
but then you loved and these two happy arms
could dream that they held only Tokubei.'
'Ohatsu say no more.' 'No, listen love,
clients have come to joy upon this breast
and have not known my eyes were shut on tears.'
`Ohatsu, if you knew how it has been.
But let me come to you, be as you were
when first in your full loveliness you lay
and the world went. It will not go as then
but for a little it will seem to go.'
    He found her waiting beautiful past thought,
himself, he could not wait. Dream and desire
worked and were eased. She smiled out of her peace,
he was come home, he should not go again.
Again, again, he loved till pleasure moaned
and cried against so great a joy. At last
rested he gazed on that surrendered grace
and the words moved in him, he had to say:
'A field of lilies all your body is,
or golden grain on which the autumn sighs
and with each sigh makes sway its plenitude.
With what kind fullness fall your lavished breasts,
looms make no silk as soft as are your sides
and Shiva's smoke lies lovely on your loins,[3]
grace grows with you and sweetness haunts your smile,

come in your calm now I can tell my tale.
But first, I never left you, always loved.
In poor Kyoto where I had to go,
poor only in the not possessing you,
lonely I wandered, longed for you and dreamt,
risen desire I saw in every flower,
in shrines the sutras I intoned became
my prayers for the One Way[4] desired, to you.
Out of day's light then most you came to me,
happy, unhappy, came to me in dreams,
the moon's bright pencil soft upon the night
traced out each lovely line and grace of you,
less form than flow as finest art should be,
and so we slept, my arm about you, dear,
till dawn's hand at my shoulder rudely woke,
vanished Ohatsu, her uplifted face
and eyes that sealed themselves to take my kiss.
No, I have never left you, always loved.'
'Dearest, there was no way for me to know.
Forgive me, I am yours, a thing you own,
your woman, call me by what name you will,
your bitch, your whore, so only that you love,
for in your arms is my heart's only home
and this used body you so highly praise
to you is given as it were my soul.'
'Ohatsu is your name, no other, dear,
it is to me as music on the strings
and you as cherryblossom on the bough
that ever moved will seem as it were still,
so is its beauty perfect in itself,
as it were not of earth, a heaven-born thing,
so you to me.' She listened to the love
more than the words and nestled to him close
the while his hand still moved and loved on her,
patient to hear some harmless, hurtless tale,
for what could touch their loves so well assured?
'Ohatsu I have done a foolish thing
and it may bear a deadly consequence.
You stare at me, "may" is not "will" as yet
though it comes close. This hand that stroking finds
you answering, that feels desire respond,
that knows so well to wake it to my will,
on you can know no acts with unsure ends,
yet such there are, elsewhere is always chance.

I have been the blind player in a game.
There was no foolishness in loving you,
yet there my griefs began - no, my dear love,
does this kiss show regret, or this, or this? -
but greatest folly in two acts well meant,
assuming all too much, two fateful acts.
Perhaps you too take harm from what you give
and all I bring is pain. The writ of law
runs fast, is not delayed, it will not wait
beyond this day. Where did it all begin?
In service, in good service, I served well
my uncle the silk merchant, he in turn,
kindly he thought, would have rewarded me
with a rich marriage. My stepmother came
and took the dowry. Ties of family
breed strongest feelings, make the most demands,
rejected hurt the most. And all this done,
no slightest word to me, what I might wish,
where my true love was set, fury I felt,
fury that grew and knew no bounds. Daily
such strife until my uncle, household head
since my dear parents' deaths, he threw me out.
"This is Ohatsu's doing", he exclaimed,
"your pretty whore, the bitch of your hot nights.
See she sings well for you this night of nights,
and for fit song that common catch they sing
along the streets, 'My love lies bleeding, all
for love of me'." So he raved on. Last fling,
"You know the law of dowries, seven days
for full repayment, and unpaid your death
a public shame, But you are kin and I
am kind. Out of your grasping mother's hands
prize it as best you can. Why would she yield
it and you not her son? So I begin
my count of days with your unwished return,
doubtless in failure, your bitch less in heat."
Such things he said, I said, that door is closed.
The same day I was on Kyoto's road.'
'But Tokubei, I would have understood,
you could have married as do other men
that find their happiness elsewhere. Babies
will busy a good wife, she knows her man
lies at another's side, she feels no love,
so there is peace at home, his duty done,[5]

his darling pleased, Marriage is not enough
or this teahouse would want for customers,
nor does this place suffice, a home completes
and one day, sad for me, will be enough.'
'Ohatsu, I am not as other men,
you speak as a mere geisha, not my wife!
The holy office we performed ourselves
in the true act of love, and were you far
in space removed but in your heart I lived
still you would be my wife. Vows we exchanged,
your silent ring speaks our true minds as then.
Others may use you in their loveless need,
still in my loving I am in my shrine
and at my worship where it most is due.
So it has been since looks of love first passed.
You know I wished you in another town
and brought to birth, our baby at your breast,
in our own home. Surely you too have dreamed
this dream and from your womb heard call our child
unborn and heeded it?'
'Oh Tokubei,
often I so have wished. What woman loves
and does not wish love's child? Yes in the act
and bliss of love fulfilled comes the desire
to breed, and the excited womb knows well
to what end its joy works. I spoke just now
as geisha but not from the heart. Dreams, dreams!
Do you not think that when you lay with me
and when you loved with me and seeded me
I held you to me with a wish for life
far dearer than my own? But, my true love,
I am but what I am, a thing for lust
to visit, sate its loveless soul upon.
Only with you has deep desire been love
and wishful of its fruit.' 'Ohatsu, no,
you are yourself and that means all to me.'
'Dearest,' she said, 'no more of dreams that hurt,
married, unmarried, we are all for use
and one good use is to give love for love.
Or find our home or not still we can love.
You come to me so I may mother you,
a crying child that tells its foolish deed
and knows the one soft breast that makes all well.'
'If I were but a child and mothering

could make this pass, your breast could well do that,
but I am not a child and mother's love,
not even yours, can put away this care.
My folly passing credence is soon told.
In my stepmother was such love of gain
hardly Kyoto's councillors had power
to loose her purse to save my father's son,
but they prevailed though after so long suit!
Of course, no more than she could they approve
of custom breached, marriages were arranged,
always had been arranged, and given time,
submission by both parties to their lot,
both brought to bed, at length a child achieved,
they worked, the most, not all. For love's free choice,
that way lay anarchy. So they opined,
but they would not let death avoidable
ensue. My hopeless case was won. Sometimes
before great loss there comes a lightening,
a lifting of the heart above all cares,
so it was, from Kyoto when I came.
    No sooner back in fair Osaka's streets
than a voice hailed me from my childish days,
then little loved, but this was a new world,
one where things worked out always for the best
whatever chance might come, a world to trust,
and the voice spoke from days of innocence.
A thriving merchant now, or so he said,
trading in oils, I told him my affairs,
he listened close. Something he had in hand
would better them. This dowry duly paid
still needs would come, yes, ever growing needs.
I thought of you, our dreams, that other town.
His 'something' was a profitable deal
that day should close, but he was short of cash,
a loan to be made good a day too late
would have saved all, perhaps I could help out?
One moment a vague thought of Providence
twice tempted came uneasily, it passed.
His seal to it, next day would see all paid,
and more! My script writ clear, all made secure,
he left me light of heart, and money too,
the money not my own! Whom gods destroy
they first make foolish with great happiness.
Since then I've searched Osaka, he is seen

about but none know where he trades or lives,
and fears crowd in on me, my time runs out.
I am indeed that crying child who seeks
the one soft breast it knows in a hard world.'
She held him to her, 'My poor Tokubei!
What is the wretch's name?' 'Kuheiji, love.'
'I know the fellow, for of late he haunts
this place, brings no kind use with him, the girls
complain, the master would be rid of him
but fears and lets all pass. I keep a knife
for such abuse, he knows and looks elsewhere.
But let us dress, go down, mealtime is near
and he may come. At least you have his seal.'
Outside they waited, watched, the land lay still
and seemed to wait with them, the wood draw near,
Kuheiji came, Tokubei caught his arm,
'The loan I made, I want that cash today.'
The rascal stared at him, 'What loan is this?',
and when good Tokubei showed script and seal
laughed loud: 'A fool's trick this, all merchants know
that seal was lost, a new one made for me
these many months ago and well before
your script's clear date. Trickster, out of my way!'
And laughing still he swept into the house.
Ohatsu said, 'You know what he has done.'
'Yes,' said her lover, 'the old seal not lost
was used on me', but he scarce heard his words,
he looked on vacancy and there he saw
the disbelieving judges doom his death,
and knew the feeling that all was deserved.
And his Ohatsu knew where his thoughts went,
and something like a cry welled in her heart
and issued in her voice for the life lost
that should have been her own, and her arms reached
to keep him hers. Slowly the words came out,
the all-accepting words, as if his doom
were hers, his way the only way to go.
'Hear me, my lover, and remember this,
Death's Mountain[6] two climb easier than one.'
And then as if the habit of her trade
still made its claim, 'A client from the shrine
of Kwannon[7] comes, and even as things are
and as I feel I go to keep my word,
as I will keep it to you this last night.

Come to me on the setting of the sun.'
She tried to smile and the house took her in.
Half heard, half heeded, she was gone, he watched,
only the arms of love then understood.
    Some time he stayed, aimless his body moved,
Through streets now emptied of all interest,
colour and life, senseless and slow he walked
the sole inhabitant of a dead town,
himself as dead. Shadows there were that smiled,
he could not smile. There was his school, the boy
that careless ran from it had never known
that those fast feet could take him otherwhere
than to his home. Walk on to the world's end?
But that was here, and how to walk away
from his sad self? In Sonezaki wood
he sat to watch the river, it went by,
what else was there to say? Beyond it dense
dark trees stood in their serried ranks to shut
him out, as if the guarded secret were
their charge, not his to reach, the answer why
to this point he was come and here an end.
He could imagine folly happy go
right to its purposed end, not turned from it
by wayside chance, so why? Upon the scene,
so long he looked at it, began to grow
a lipless, eyeless face of shifting leaves,
forming, dissolving and reforming still,
a face that knew his question from of old
and listened out of silence so well kept.
    And it was then as he near entered in
that silence to be still, and of the wood
and water made a part, the speaking face
of his Ohatsu came, her words half lost
but one thing clear, to come as the sun set,
and it was setting now for him, his world.
What splendours in the dying of a sun!
He turned from it and went towards the house.
It was the same bright scene as other nights,
yet not the same, the life so far from him:
on cushions loud the talking laughing men,
girls with their painted fans, like butterflies
endless in movement, caught, pulled down on laps,
the question put, the two upon the stairs.
He toyed with food, time came and sat with him

and the scene seemed to waver, pass from sight.
No, he could see Ohatsu bright in talk
signal with nod and smile and turn alone
to take the steps, stately tonight and sweet,
golden kimono circled with blue sash,
his gifts like all her garments, so her wear
his dreams. A while he waited, followed her.
At once arms laced his neck, cheek met his cheek,
so loved his world awoke, he lived again,
at last came clear the half heard words, and tears
welled in his heart and gathered to his eyes
in thinking on the gift that they had meant,
of all her gifts the greatest, undeserved.
Words there were to be said but love came first,
and on this night so unlike other nights
as meaning more for what would come of it,
so was their loving unlike all before,
this night love was religion and a rite
and she the priestess at its ordering.
The geisha's white she had washed from her face,
for flesh that loved and died was to be paid
its due devotions, not in its own kind
but with the touch of eyes. First she undressed
him, giving oftentimes the lightest kiss,
as he did her, his stroke a reverence,
and so they knelt each other worshipping.
His body was to her a holy thing,
as hers to him, remembrance tendering
of many sweet encounters, loving joys.
Once in her giving she had said to him,
'I am your house of love and in me are
rooms many readied for your visiting,
and in each one a bed is kept for you
where I am laid and waiting for your love.'
After this night would be nor room, nor bed,
no waiting for his visiting. So much
she had to give that he would never take.
She looked on strength of shoulders, strength of loins
that on her should have had the fathering
of sons and daughters now with the unborn,
and a long moment the bright eyes were blind;
on arms held still that with such tenderness
had taken her so often to his use
and her submitted body brought to bliss,

the hands that moved with such a gentleness
as only love can use, and made her know
herself its subject with each touch and stroke.
All this she saw and more, but most her loss.
Death's shadow on him made him beautiful.
    And he, beauty and more he saw in her,
the spirit in the body visible,
made one with it. Ohatsu as now seen,
no other at the end he would recall:
the dark head bowed above her loveliness
as if all were too slight an offering
to her love's lord; the folded hands that might
become a supplicant, not such as she,
the bringer of great gifts; dark-lidded eyes
that lowered yet shone out so clear and bright;
lips red-ripe for the kissing, summer lips,
though seeing them he felt their season pass;
the breasts of her compassion that he saw
as two pale pendants with rich rubies tipped;
her woman's body promising such joy
that one day they had hoped would bear his son.
And suddenly he wept and held to her,
and the two held together, her head bent
like a flower laden with the evening's dew
discharging its moist burden silently.
    So the two mourned, wordless and close they mourned,
until she took his hands in hers and said:
'Now, my beloved, is our time to talk.
Tonight Death's Mountain sees us handed climb,
step from the top into the Sleep and Dawn,
perhaps wake on one lotus,[8] turn and smile,
know other loves and sweeter than are here,
children it may be come from me as kind
and easy as the Spring brings forth its flowers
in its full time, which is the gentle sun's.
If not, still you will be my own great child
forever at my side.' 'Ohatsu, these
are pretty fancies suiting a dear heart.
Death is most terrible, not pretty, nor
easy its coming, though companioned well,
and least self-death. And after, who can say?
And yet on midnight's stroke I wait, and know
I should not wait but go and go alone.
You have so much of life, the new day's hope

in you is radiant, so as you pass
men talking leave to talk and turn and stare,
feel their cares sit more light for that bright hope,
some gently touch as if that passing life
could flow to them, your unresenting smile
the day's best sweetener. They if you came
would say, "What waste that face of beauty lost,
she was meant for the sun!" Say nothing now,
think long on it.' Silent the two embraced,
silent they dressed, yet at the door he turned,
'In Sonezaki wood there is no sun.'

Ohatsu did not rest, she paced her room,
thought of the many men, their use of her,
hunger at home that sold her to that use,[9]
the day her father took her to the town
and to the house where pleasure was her work.
Pleasure at first, she learned to dance and sing,
move gracefully, converse, all ways to please,
the sum of many skills the art of love.
She had enjoyed her custom of delight,
even been proud to make so prized a gift.
And then the weariness of use set in,
she acted out her given part of joy,
her moment real but all volitionless.
And more and more her self would be withdrawn,
her body made a puppet to desire,
the lover's such another; she would watch
from some far place, removed, indifferent,
the puppeteer, the puppets, all perform
their antic movements, creatures of the play.
And sometimes in her arms strange pity moved
for men, all children, lips went to the breast.

And then came Tokubei, for the first time
she longed for arms that held her as herself,
to lie and look into an inner sky
at what they both called love, then turn to love
and to be loved, meet his desire with hers.
These were the days of glad imagining,
he came a lover to her bed and stayed
a husband with his rights in her, his ring
upon her finger, and it went unsaid,
they both dreamt babies and a home for them.
What had she said, 'I am but what I am,'
geisha, no more. But that was never true,

and least since Tokubei took her to wife.
Wife that night she would prove. His love said stay
yet wished her by his side as wife should be.
This was a land of marriages arranged
and lovers who made pacts of suicide,
faithful in death, and she could love no less.
'There is no more to say,' she told her ring,
'it was all said the day he put you on,'
and her mind set, lay down to wait the hour.
    It was near midnight when Ohatsu rose,
dressed herself in the black a bride should wear[10]
chose a white obi, she would make death proud,
looked for the last time on her whore's soft bed,
and yet the same where in their private world
she dreamed with Tokubei, where he had said
'I love you', and she knew that he spoke true.
And now in darkness on a step she stood
and listened to the house. It talked to her,
asked her what she did there, why go to him?
And with that question she was in love's arms
and all the answers known. Another step,
six more, and then the way to the barred door
clear but for the one watch, a servant-girl
above whose nodding head huge shadows leapt,
the light before her wildly flickering.
Ohatsu, wide sleeve flying in her haste,
brushed the lamp from its stand, the frighted girl
groped for a flint, the master's voice was heard,
frantic, Ohatsu reached the door and with
her last of strength unbarred it, and near fell
into the waiting arms of Tokubei.
    Hurried, her one thought flight, past shapes half seen
that seemed to flee with her, to the path dark
along Osaka's tree-lined riverbank,
dark save where pools of light the moon let spill
at open intervals, she had to stop
and lean on him to ease her laboured breath.
He said, 'Listen, our River of Three Ways,[11]
now we are come to Sonezaki wood',
and the names sounded in her ears as one,
as Journey's End, and she was come to it.
Voices upon the water came to them,
high women's laughter on the night air borne,
now loud, now faint, lost intermittently;

distant the coloured lanterns swayed on trees,
a pleasure-house much as her own had been,
but open to all hours for visiting
the girls were worn with work, age came too soon.
She thought how the years might have dealt with her,
the lines of wear. Handed they stood and looked
to lights and life so far from their intent.
He had been there, some unremembered girl.
    'This world goes on,' she said, 'tomorrow they
will talk and laugh, some few will say of us,
"From the far side of dark Umeda Bridge[12]
they look back shadows that once people were",
and then forget us as the world forgets.
What else? As now I would forget myself.'
Her arms went round him and by one consent
they sought the earth and kind oblivion.
Night with its stars for their bed's canopy,
the moon-blanched trees for closest curtaining,
the water for still burden to love's song,
her beauty to the moon and him full bared,
she lay to feel his tender fingering
as on an instrument he loved to play
and wake to its full power of harmony.
And yet the fingers stilled, the music stayed
just as it had begun so movingly.
    Instead upon the silence came his voice:
'This is our last of love, as last of nights,
you wear my ring, the moon shines bright on it,
but brighter, sweeter far to me the thought
that I have worn you as you wear my ring
so many loving times, and in my life
most valued you for jewel.' 'Even as I
have valued you,' she said. And on these words
the music recommenced, she felt it rise,
soar and ascend above the night, herself,
to climax full, and on the top of it
heard her glad cry. Where he had taken her
no one could stay, yet still in their descent
the tune played on, lingered in memory.
He had not moved from her, his hand stroked on.
Quiet she lay still hearing what she'd heard
if fainter now, their last and best of love.
    Round them the many voices of the night
were one, within them and of happiness,

peace lay upon her, its lips to her lips,
the world was in her arms, if just for then.
But joy not long forgets its opposite,
rather recalls, and suddenly she wept.
That grey thought death, so desolate, was come,
a minute past forgotten it had slept
quite out of mind, but here it was again
with all it meant. He held her as she said:
'The thing that hurts is to have so much love
and not to ease it giving of itself.
When you were sad I should have comforted,
when happy, happy been for you and more,
your house more than a house have been your home,
the slippers that I fetched been fetched with love,[13]
loving I should have been so big by you,
such children born, but death makes barren wombs.'
So she could grieve yet say what brought them there,
'But we have loved.' He kissed her gathered breasts,
'One child you had, myself, and mothered him
even to this', and he could say no more.
He raised her from the earth where they had loved,
her tied kimono with his hand brushed down,
a needless gesture now it might be thought
but even such slight loving brought some ease
and death like life should have its decent dress.
    One duty stayed and they remembered it,
prayer for her parents, for his uncle he,
though it might seem little was owing them,
but praying helped, strange peace and calm was theirs
and the determined spirit moved in them.
Her voice came clear to him, 'Where do we die?'
And he, as if another spoke in him:
'Here was our best and last of love so here.
See how this palm outspread is to that pine
and close they twine, so you as my spread palm
with me your pine together kindly came
and were as one and one will be in death.'[14]
Quiet the river ran, Ohatsu said:
'Our necks have rivers where the lifeblood runs
and delicate the banks containing them,
cut these the life runs out. Use your knife well,
this from my sleeve then ends your agony.'
    'Love, my Ohatsu, as you close your eyes
in sign to strike it will be then I die,

but there are things to do before that time.
My gift, your obi, cut it first in two,
sad use so different from what we knew
when first you tied it and untied for me.
Now is your beauty all unbound, cut free.
With one length thus I bind you to the palm
and with the other bind me to the pine,
so we may moveless stay and side by side,
some walker in the sun see us and say,
"Death did not part them that love so made one."
There, it is done.' Close, close the lovers came
in long embrace. 'Come soon, my love,' she said
and closed her eyes. His was the harder part,
twice the blade turned aside, despairing and
in tears blindly he struck, the point went home
and to his shoulder her head bowed, it fell.
He gave himself no time. Whether it were
by nature or by some great act of will
his own head turned and rested upon hers.
So all that night they stayed as they had meant.
    There is a shrine in Sonezaki wood
where still true lovers come and kneel and pray
that they may know togetherness as these,
like them together enter in the One.

Notes:

1 A remaking of Chikamatsu Monzaemon's tale in his puppet play, The Love Suicides of Sonezaki 1703. Geisha were housed, used, in such places, and on professional occasions appeared as at '2'.

3 In a Sanskrit poem the lover is Vishnu, Destroyer and Fire-god chasing the god of love into his beloved's womb, the smoke of his passage is her beautiful vaginal hair.

4 The One Way is Buddha's way of life.

5 Such peaceable arrangements are said to be still in use.

6 A mountain in the Japanese afterworld.

7 A Buddhist saint.

8 One of the prettier fancies of Japanese Buddhism and is in the play.

9 Such sale was not uncommon, for the girl an honourable sacrifice.

10 Black is the bride's wear, often with contrasting white beneath. The obi is the kimono's sash with large knot. Death is the bridegroom here.

11 The river in Japanese Buddhism corresponding to the Greek river Styx across which the dead went to Hades.

12 There is an Umeda station in Osaka. The bridge is dark because conceived as a way to death.

13 This wifely practice is still known in Japan.

14 The conceit of the trees and main details of the death are in Monzaemon's play, otherwise treatment of the story is this author's.

INNOCENTS

In Old Japan it was, then not yet one,
in fair Kyoto for its gardens famed
and alleys bright with cherry blossom hung,
Kyoto of the blossoms as men say,
its consequence among the far seen hills
where comes the morning sun, clear visitor,
its time when this rich region kept the law
of property and therefore marriage rights
in ancient force and strict as nowhere else,
a moment's folly, love beyond regret.[1]
    From this fair town a merchant traded forth
and when he did left his good clerk in charge,
in one respect a perfect innocent,
he never haunted Flowers, their scented beds,
preferring day's work done to walk the lanes
tree-lined and dream upon the shadowed lakes.
As for the merchant, senses satisfied
in the Flower Quarter he went home to sleep,[2]
not wake his wife with foolish fond demands.
What should she know of the fine arts of love,
rare services his darling did for him?
No, let her keep his house, do wifely chores.
Why had he married? It was use and wont,
for the near teahouse better served day's needs,
the cheerful talk, the pretty chambered girls.
Children he wanted none, such squalling brats,
and costly too like-minded friends would say.
So, innocent enforced his wife must live
a dream of days and nights none different,
a model of dull domesticity.
And yet a rebel hid, a gamesome mind
that fled of nights with fleeting faceless shapes.
If once one would come closer, live and love!
    A call came from the north, a noble there

whose word was not to be gainsayed, nor wealth,
would see fine silks, hear fashions, it would mean
months of rough travel, but the profits more
than counterweighed the pains. His love must wait,
he must forgo, so much he must forgo,
a thigh so pillow-soft, a singing voice
the sweetest, winning thoughts from merchandise,
and the slow dance, hands plump yet delicate
outlining the full body of her grace,
and then, and then, herself, the thought of that
made small all losses else. He sighed, along
his way Flowers there would be, but none like her.

The merchant's going made but little stir,
his geisha had more clients to delight,
the clerk scarce noticed, used to handling things,
the wife found life the dream it always was,
though just of late the nights had brought one face
that came a little closer, almost known,
a lover but the features stayed unclear.
Yet once that gamesome spirit moved. The clerk
was all that made days drab, alike, unlived.
He came and talked accounts, well veiled[3] she heard,
once as he went had raised the veil, confused
had met his steady eyes, she was not there.
King in his counting-house, so self-contained,
surely this paragon must sometimes think
on other figures than are found in books.
Married or single all men had their loves,
that was the way of things. He loved himself!
She could not see those eyes look lovingly.
Quite personable, handsome some might say,
expression bright, nose, lips, so sensitive,
his ledger was his life. The proverb ran,
as fire to flax so woman to the man.
Then might be seen the man one never knew,
and least himself. Well, she would test its truth.

Of course, no loving, just a minute's sport,
that one wild moment wake him, make him think
one of her maidens waited, sick for love
of his so perfect self, then suddenly
appalled at her bold deed fled through the night.
Days he would scan each face to know that love,
even her own, but little there he'd find!
Oh she could see it all, a comedy.

He'd work till dark, then faithful to his hour
seek the small room and dimly netted couch,
see there a woman's shape, true woman's shape,
rounded and full as woman ought to be,
and seeing so excitedly undress,
his fingers foolish, while she sped her way
leaving a baffled and bewildered clerk.
Almost she could be sorry for the man.
    Or so she planned, the clerk came late, she slept,
as gentle as a kiss he took her there,
and still she slept, even when once she cried,
it was her dream-love come, but closer now,
light his lips on her lips and light his hands.
So to dream ever, wake to memory!
Only when morning came she knew her case,
this was the clerk's bed, he'd made love to her,
her night-wear was dishevelled, sash untied.
And she was desperate, he could not tell,
but if with this night's loving she conceived!
Who would believe her? No man, not the law,
and the bright sword of justice would descend.
Wives must keep faith while husbands slept abroad,
life could be so unfair. Certain by now
some household eye had noted her made bed
unslept in, watched to see her leave this door.
It was an age before she reached her room,
her maid was there, did the eyes question her?
    And a like desperation seized the clerk.
What had possessed him? He had seen her face
shut in so innocent and sweet a sleep,
given so wholly to its dream, folded
a flower in night's dark bed, and he had spoiled
its beauty like a thief, no, murderer,
all his so well masked love released in rape!
And more, as the accusing dawn had shown,
the bloody spoiler of virginity.
No matter why he found her where she lay -
some household search and overtaking sleep? -
her honour and his trust were lost, quite lost.
From his returning master he could hope
no silent mercy, worse still nor could she.
They met with lowered eyes and nothing said.
    Love is the oddest thing, so diversely
motived, set on, and the most luckless chance

that should give caution and diminish may
increase to ever growing, in this case
love grew with fear. Now the clear figures blurred,
helpless he watched his hand move of itself
and the one woman's face come from his pen,
nor did he see his drawing, only her,
so beautiful and doomed. Sometimes alone
she stood in a dark alley swept by trees,
all pale and pleading while red blossoms rained,
unnatural! Sometimes a sword was sketched
above her neck and the tall headsman wept
great tears of blood. The red ink from his pen
flowed terribly. These nights his lamp burned late.
    And as for her, strange lassitude would take
her mind and limbs, her hands would stroke her thighs
as if its source were there, not all in fear,
though that could stay her step, lift hand to heart
fast beating in her breast, so clear death's scene,
and in her room alone make her cry out.
Her bed, no more her bed, gave her no rest,
she had to find a refuge from herself.
And so it was on such a stressful night,
heart louder than her step, she found herself
moving by lightless ways to the one door
that held an equal knowledge of her state,
waiting an endless minute, entering.
He sat upon his bed, to the warm night
quite bare, head on his hands, looking on space
as if from the one thought he could not move,
and she was almost to him when he stirred.
He stood and stared, held out his arms to her.
Scarce knowing what she did she entered them,
and on his breast felt hand go to her head
and to her side, and as his stroke still came
scarce knew her sash untied, herself undressed
and gently laid beside him to be loved,
knew only this was where she had to be.
    Her tears he kissed away, kissed everywhere,
his closeness comforted, the sobbing stilled,
and sometime they were one, peace wanted came
and did not go, always each would be there
to meet the other's need. Her man, his wife,
the night had made them so. He said to her,
'I took from you what was a husband's right,

but it is this night truly married us.
Love its own ceremony is and seals
the action of our loving, you are mine
and made my care.' Fear's fingers still could touch,
but then he held her as if he would ward
her from all harms and she believed he could.
The dreadful lightning now of the bright sword
fell hurtless, moved away. At last she slept,
his gentle kiss unfelt. Now without fail
openly, recklessly, she came to him,
made their loves his concern. Was she not his?
    And so he thought, yes, they were his concern
and she was his, and if he were to keep
her they must flee. The days spoke flight to him,
the nights urged haste, and still a month or more
he had to wait till certain sums were paid,
demands were met that unmet when they fled
would have meant hue and cry. Accounts left fair
could mean pursuit delayed. Meantime they loved.
Talk of love hidden, feelings, dreams by her
so much misread that at the last they led
her to an act of folly, folly shared,
and all the loving that had come of it
each night renewed, was a sweet interlude
before their play's main act; they must ensure
their lives and loves together and go forth
to find their place, the home that she would make.
Came the night when he said: 'The morrow's sun
lighting the high hills has to see us there.
Dress now, my love, provide as best you can,
we have no little way to go.' She went
upon his kiss and, his pack shouldered full,
two handed shadows fled their moonlit way.
    High in the hills by paths the loneliest
come with a tiring step, and sore for her
though held by his strong arm, at last they stood
and looked on space, the miles and miles of it,
the sunlit uplands seeming set in it
as freedom's boundless element, as vast
as time itself. The little that they asked,
so much to them, lay somewhere there, a home.
In that spread vastness they might well be lost
and safe from all pursuit. Her spirits rose,
surely life would provide for life, its own,

and to her womb not showing yet she clasped
his all unknowing hand, so glad, and laughed
when on her sudden kiss his look asked why.
But he must not know yet, not now the time
to tell him, see his father's face light up,
later would be a time, their aim in sight
and he the less concerned for their lives saved.
    That all too high, too early, spirits soared
and he had reason for concern appeared
their tenth day out, the feet of horse were heard.
At once he looked for cover, not far off
under stones heaped had burrowed vagrant hands
to make a shelter, leaving piled a roof.
He seized her hand, breathless she ran with him,
hidden they watched slow canter, strong of breast
and limb, a force of mountain ponies, search
was meant, most like for them, but they passed on.
Fear shook her like an ague, in his arms
went slow from her. He found his stroking grow
desirous and she answered his desire,
fear wanting reassurance yet more close.
That she was his and safe was all her thought,
and it was good to be so taken, all
fear put away, give place to soaring joy.
After, he smoothed her dresses down,[4] 'We go
on as before, they will look otherwhere.'
And tired in one embrace they slept. Morning
saw their way clear, they kissed, careful went on.
    They passed a woodsman's hut, quite bare
of life he thought, but an old woman showed,
small and thin-faced, hands twisted sore, bright-eyed.
'You are the runaways,' she said, 'the hunt
is for. I will not tell them, though my man
would speak. Fools' gold is all he craves and he
is gone their guide. Trust me, they will beat back
as forward, every covert searched for you
till they are sure the birds haunt other ways,
then they will beat there too. They seek fools' gold,
as blind as he. They will win nothing. Just
a word on duty and so forth. The Court-
men, Samurai, the law, know little of,
care less for, the poor folk, their driven beasts.
You wonder why I help?' She crooked at them
a sore bent finger, 'Hate, hate for my man,

these woods, this life. See how my tongue
runs on. Once I could say, as your joined hands
now say, that there is love. Once I could think
he knew it, I was wrong.' Tears filled old eyes,
All he could do was wordless take her hand.
'Old fool! Old fool!,' she said, 'but if you knew
why I could come with him to these lone parts,
the reason long since gone!' And then, 'Surely
you see that never will you two, and what
she -', but a finger at his woman's lips
silenced her there.
'A word with her,' she said,
and led her in. 'He does not know? Of course,
then he would go more slow, and for its sake
all must be tried. Years can make you forget
even what nature once so simply said.
But the way is so hard.' 'I stay with him,'
she answered. 'Yes, I understand, you love.
Then take my blessing,' and they kissed, went out.
To him, 'See yon high hill, make that your mark
and go about it. Horse will never climb,
and if you pass it, so unlikely, safe.'
He knew but nodded thanks. 'But not till then.'
Some time she watched them go, you might have said
clasped hands were raised in prayer, then slow went in.
'What did she want?' he asked. 'I think it was
just to be with a woman, no man there,
if for a minute. And she cared, danger
was on those mountain paths for untried feet.'
So she still put him off. He only said,
'Not dangerous as are the ways of men.'
She wondered, did old eyes see all that much?
Days passed in long ascents, descents, till one
midmorn they came upon a little lake,
the sun burning out of a blue that lent
its colour to the snowy tops of hills
and to the water, clear, inviting them,
a mirror to its world. They stopped and stripped,
she glad for all her many garments gone.
In that great quiet cries and laughter rang,
so unforeseen the cold, sharp shock of it,
and threshing to the shore they ran and ran
till heat so sudden lost returned to them,
and on the green bank laughing down they fell,

rested a space and for each other reached.
    Never had life cried quite so loud in them,
never desire with such sweet tongues had sung
its instant need, the beauty of love made.
It was as if some giant hand laid hold,
lifted them to a country yet unknown,
glimpsed from afar, then only fitfully,
or visited but not as now to live,
the first of men and women to explore.
They had not left their earth but so it felt,
in full surrender one delighted soul.
After, they lay and the great valley seemed
scarce space and room enough for so great peace.
Then unexpectedly, near sadly said
by her, 'I think no happiness like this
comes after.' Silent he could feel the same.
Locked in each other's arms the lovers slept.
    It was near noon when the two sleepers stirred
and to his waking eyes her naked grace
showed native, natural as any flower
the valley grew. Her smile returned his love.
They ate, held hands, the moveless water was
the face of that clear peace their spirits knew,
and the reflected heights that soaring joy
so lately shared. 'Husband,' she asked of him,
for by all tokens of their love he was,
'are we not on our way to safety yet?
Days we have journeyed and Kyoto seems
a dream of other lives, a dress thrown by.'
'Upon our way, but we have not arrived.
Still I fear eyes on us, tongues that report.'
And yet her talk of dress thrown by came back
and the idea came. 'Sweetheart,' he said,
'this little lake you will remember it,
here we made love as in another world,
here to that other world we found the way.
    'Past yon green mountain by used paths we go
in country guise unnoted. There search stops,
no jealous law such as we flee from here
has force, and none in village or in town
even if found would stir to send us back.
But first to win our wear. Here naked need
must help, for in these hills I mean to find
a cottage, beg a night's bed and rude dress.

In that first moment seen, when nature speaks,
we may win all, with morn be on our way,
though afterthoughts will come in dangerous
and be what custom says. What they do then
too well I guess, most like they follow us
on expert feet and overtake, the chance
I dread. But I must act, for you, for us.'
Gone was that peace they knew, so lately knew,
and knowing all his thought and how he felt
she drew him down on her, as if in her
were the one answer to all cares and doubts,
the answer her great love, 'But I am yours
and where you go there will I also go.'
A while he had no words, silent they loved
and all their loving done sober he said:

'Two things we do. First some part of our wear[5]
we cast about, so hunters finding it
will say "love's suicides" and not unmoved
give up the chase, while safely we go on.
Second, with what clothes left we go where no
sun warms, but cold winds bite at you, and when
as the dark deepens and our mountain looms
the hoped for cottage glimmers, there, in sight
of it, in that so cutting cold we strip,
go naked to the door. We were waylaid,
lost all. Then our so plain distress must speak.
There your bowed head, bared beauty, folded hands,
will better plead our case than all my words.'
Each cast some clothes, he said, 'So much to ask.'
Her only answer was to take his hand
and with him go, hoping but loving more.

It was some way along a moorland path,
the sun still felt, and even if footsore
the lovers glad for the yet windless air,
out of a silence the clerk spoke: 'You knew
me first as a man sealed to work, alone,
without or gift, or wish for company.
I talked, yes, but it was not I who talked,
all in the way of business my few words.
Such busy shadows all my converse with!
And of them I was one, as shadowlike.
And then you came into my ken. One day
I saw you as yourself, lovely, alive.
I had not seen your face but heard your voice,

and your full figure spoke, "I could be kind",
said it with breast and hip, each movement made.
Without my meaning love I was in love,
dull days now had an aim, I looked for you.
I could be more than pleased some geisha bound
your master's senses in so strong a spell,
leaving your beauty all unhusbanded.
Dreams made you mine and could not stay mere dreams
that night I found you in my bed. Your dream
I was to learn, though all unknowingly
had been of me. Dearest,' he stopped and held,
as if so only he could fetch from him
that perfect soul of utterance he sought,
'What I would say is that real life is love
and without love is only shadow-life,
true love is a possession unto death
and were you dead would live beyond. My love,
all of me that is real cries out, "I love".
Yes if death came to us goodbye said then
could only mean to us a long goodnight,
love that had been still would have been, my love.'
Bright tears said all she felt, as did her kiss.

So they strove onwards, the wind rose, between
great rocks, in some more sheltered hollow he
would try with press of bodies to bring warmth,
but the light soon must show. It showed, they stripped,
near crying the pair shivered at a door
bleak under mountain shadows, where few goats
and lean cropped a spare grass, told their set tale.
An old man lonely did not keep them there.
No matter true or false, their need was plain.
He saw the woman shamed so to be seen,
cringing before the wind, and beautiful,
the man grim-faced in his concern for her.
Suspicion set aside he said, 'Come in,'
laid wood upon a hearth still smouldering
and made it blaze. They pressed close as they could.
Garments of his dead wife he fetched for her,
coarse on a tender skin that had known silk,
tight against breasts and belly such as hers,
at least a covering; and for the man
wear welcome though as coarse left by the son
long since lost to the towns, for both his guests
the warming dish they craved. And as they ate

heard their tale through, north-bound and stripped of all
by ruffians. More kind than credulous
to his known peace violence in the hills
believed or not was an exciting thought,
and voices telling it rare company.
Too soon he had to show them to their rest.
    Bedded in a bare loft, alone at last,
two threadbare blankets between them and night,
still cold the lovers lay, but soon undressed
knowing how best to make warmth come to them,
their blood flowed fast, they were themselves again.
Some time that night in her relief she told
him of the life she carried, and in awe
he laid his head to hear the little heart
still faint yet heard. 'Our child!', he said, and then
as tenderly as if herself the child
held her to him until through tears she laughed,
'But I have months to go, love me, my love.'
That night in the bare loft great joy was theirs.
The old man from below heard them and smiled,
and as he passed to sleep dreamt of the day
he brought a young wife to his house and bed.
    But tiredness was upon them, they too slept,
she first, he staring into a strange night
of feelings new to him, new joy, new care,
and he went dreaming a scene set by them:
behind closed eyes he saw a sunshine path
he knew to be the mountain's, onwards bright
a child, part of the sunshine, danced between
them, lightly holding to his hand, her hand,
behind a cloud of darkness raced their way,
the child broke off, ran back, near lost in it.
Running to fetch it he awoke afraid,
but she slept sound, her head within his arm
and in a moment he slept quite as sound.
    Dawn saw them on their way with many thanks
and a light step, though still they looked
about as if all went too well. Handed they walked
into the sun, together as for life.
A passer-by unheeding cheered still more.
They had a feeling of great happiness,
impossible but theirs. Each minute face
would turn to face and all it saw was dear,
terribly dear, and for the life she bore.

They were into the foothills now, near safe
from knowledge and from reach of their own kind.
The ground was stony here and goat-skin shoes
their host had given proved their usefulness.
He had felt more than paid by her quick kiss.
Another day should see them where they aimed,
within the limits of their wished for land.
That night they huddled between two great stones
and waited sleeping, sleepless, for the dawn.
    But dawn is not day's end that calls us home,
and that same night the old man had gone down
to the next village, glad of news to tell
and of the audience so seldom his,
so little men who knew the world, they thought,
heeded his simple tales out of the hills,
his still more simple sayings from a life
that had known sadness, lonely days his lot.
This once the inn was silent as he talked:
'Lovers they were as all looks, deeds, made plain,
their frequent touching past a married use,
and doubtless runaways. And what man heard
of robbers in these parts, poor as we are?
Old eyes could see the woman was with child.
Naked they came, out of a storybook!
What suffering, out of the night so come,
must they have known! I took them in, their wants
supplied, and morning saw them handed go.
The story past their story who should know?
I did not ask, they were just folk in need
and very much in love.'
    Pleased with himself,
his argument, attention so entire,
his story told, the herdsman looked around,
scanned the hard ring of faces turned on him,
caught the fierce glint in eyes he thought he knew,
and of a sudden wished his words unsaid.
He should have known, he was an innocent,
the need, the love, said nothing, strangeness did,
in their harsh calendar of the year's crimes
departure from used ways came always first
and worst. Almost he heard his dead wife's voice,
'Old fool, you talk too much.' A villager
had heard of such a pair, of late thought dead
for scattered clothes along a lakeside found,

a faithless wife with too well witnessed guilt,
a clerk from a respected master fled.
    The hunt was on in this room even now,
'just folk in need' were words to jeer at, as
their user too, who for his sympathy
was seen almost accomplice in the crime.
He sat neglected, heard the crowd-voice rise,
saw the pair in their need and love last night,
wanted to shout, 'I liked them, they had life,'
and cursed his vain tale-telling tongue
that had set all this hate afoot. Come light
well practised feet would find the fugitives,
then they, their child, and there thought stopped. No! No!
He rose, no one looked when the old man left,
he was dispensable. The street was bare
but clear and clean under the moon, and past
its end he turned into the hills. Not fleet
of foot like some he left, he knew each path
and part like none of them, so he went on.
    So little sleep had come to them at last
the lovers had gone on, though slow they went.
A moonlit height now showed their near approach
to freedom, but near meant as the eye saw,
at this rate they would be unfree, and far
from the aimed mark when the sun rose, and they
were unsure of their way. A shadow moved,
the old man walked to them, 'Hunters will come
at dawn, trust me and follow close.' He went,
stepping where shadows only seemed to be,
they learned to trust him. Night-hour on night-hour
will kept her moving and her lover's arm.
At last they stopped beside the marking-stone,
the dawn had broken and they saw their land.
'Freedom you gave us,' the clerk said, 'but why?'
'I owed it,' said the herdsman. 'Ask no more.'
She kissed him, 'I am paid,' and he turned back.
    He found the hunters waiting. 'Why?' one asked.
He pointed to the pair near lost to sight,
'For them, there is too little love, I could
not let you kill them and love's child. Never.'
'You know the consequence?' 'Yes, but I have
outlived myself and they begin to live.'

Notes:

1 There is such a moment in Saikaku's 'Almanac Maker' 1686 but not of love. The characters are unattractive, know what they are doing. This tale is mostly my invention.

2 The quarter for geisha and prostitute.

3 A woman was meant to be seen only by her husband.

4 The women of early Japan seem to have worn voluminous clothes to hide the figure.

5 Saikaku has this device for his loveless fugitives, no more.

THE GO-BETWEEN[1]

On the verandah Genji sat and smiled
over the heads of the two talking boys -
boys as he saw them, sadly he was now
in his late forties - at pink-blossom lawns.
Fragility, and youth a blossom borne,
he could not help but feel it. Such blue skies!
His good son Yūguri, Kashīwagi,
son of his oldest friend Tō no Chujō,
they talked as if they would be shocked to hear
someone could think the football match just played[2]
of less importance than some other things,
women, the court. And this was as should be,
but not for him, Genji 'the Shining One'
for the bright radiance his presence cast
on company, the smile that overcame
all difference and dissidence, Genji
so competent in business and in love.
So many his affairs, yet he had cared
and any word of need, misfortune, saw
the loved beneath the shelter of his roof,
happy in the kind keeping of his arms.
Many his ladies, children felt too few
to give his love to in a world where love
was life's best gift, they with most need of it.
    The thought went out past the unending lawns,
moved with the small white clouds in that blue sky,
painfully, overwhelmingly, he felt
the fleeting years, envied the young men there
touched only by the present it would seem.
Was it this sense of transience that made
him so love women, wish one more with child,
and not decline the Princess offered him?
Did the young body that would burgeon well
speak to him then? Yet he had kept away.
His old love Murasaki, barren, ill,
and still so beautiful, meant so much more.
There must be order, loyalties came first.
    And something now said by Kashīwagi
chimed with that sober thought, a football team
had its own kind of music, seen, not heard,
ball passed from waiting foot to waiting foot,
the play moved on. So instrument replied

to instrument, sounds passing still about
but ever onward to the closing chord.
Good Yūguri found the comparison
too fanciful, and yet, his father thought,
nature asked harmony, that lost, all lost.
The Princess troubled him, had harmony
been broken in the plain disparity of years
or would desire in her supply the breach?
Kashīwagi, not all was harmony
in that young man, fell into silences,
and then the very soul of company.
A flower could move him, women not at all,
his dash and enterprise he had just proved.
In love perhaps tender and violent?
    And as the Shining One smiled down and thought
came a commotion from not far behind,
from the pavilion of the ladies who
still watched and lingered at their slitted screens.
Movement seemed to erupt, fighting its string
a small black figure raced and a screen fell,
the boys had risen and Kashīwagi
felt more than saw the leap into his arms
of a black cat. His eyes were on the girl
that stayed and gazed while other women fled.
A childlike face yet live with quiet charm,
lovely and still, naively curious
about so fair a world, and men in it,
as if all were a painted scene admired,
then she was gone. He grew at last aware
of Yūguri so angry at his side,
both with the woman and his sight of her,[3]
and turned his full attention to the cat
now purring loudly and in great content.
It was the woman's, he was sure of it,
why he could not have said, but certain she
was beautiful. 'Sir,' he said, 'it would seem
this cat has chosen me, I should be glad
of it for company, could it be mine?'
Genji smiled lazily. 'Someone will learn
a lesson by her loss. Yes, it is yours,'
and he was thinking, a too lonely youth.
    But in his room stroking, Kashīwagi
was with the vision seen, and dreaming so
it was no cat he stroked, but softer far

the body of a girl. He should not think
this way he knew, and did. His hand stroked on,
but would she find it pleasurable as
this creature that could change its loyalty
so easily? Was this how love could come,
immediately and where it never should?
For he admired, respected Genji and
the Shining One had been so kind to him,
and Yūguri close friend, who read too well
his captive gaze. And for all that he saw
her now, so unaware until she felt
his eyes on her, the fall of hair so long
his hand would have liked well to linger on,
the face that finger-tips alone should touch,
so like a flower it was. Yes, he could see
the robe of red with lavender pale-lined,
the cloak of white with gold clasps at the neck,
the many-coloured sleeves, the blush of fear.
You could be awed by Genji, mild and kind
as his so brilliant self would seem. A rush
of blood indignant coursed him that young years
should feel the hands of age on them. Could he
want interest as it was said? Did he
not sleep with her? 'Let it be so,' he prayed
hands clenched, 'let it be so O Blessed One.'
    He could not boldly walk into, invade,
the women's quarters, seek her room and say
outside her curtained bed all that he felt,
as lovers elsewhere had been known to do,
yet she must know. And then it came to him,
the lady Kojiju waited on her,
a woman not of any rank, he had
seen her at court a servant, and met her
each time he visited the home of his
old nurse her mother. Then she brought the tea,
said little, a quite ordinary girl
but pleasant looking, and her greeting smile
had a great sweetness. Would she help him now?
He visited her home, she heard him out
and briefly she refused. 'Only a note,'
he said, 'it may amuse and you can read.
She can reject, but she will know of me
and that I am in love, hopeless or not.'
He took her hand, 'You have been dear to me

and this should bring us closer. Think again.'
'You saw her,' she replied, 'and Genji was
greatly displeased, I heard him speak of it.
His women are for his eyes only. She
is but a child and the byways of love
Genji has walked so happily
and with him all his ladies, they are full
of fear for her. You will win no reply.
You ask in the wrong quarter to be sad
and she distressed, yet I will speak for you.'
He kissed her, did not hear her say, 'Now am
I one unhappy lady, love makes use of me.'
    The Princess read the words, knew what they meant,
        'The black cat that I stroke, it is not mine,
        but these so lonely hands still they must stroke.'
She knew him, yes, the player on the field,
the young man seen to talk so earnestly,
whose eyes met hers so disconcertingly
above the cat there cradled in his arms.
Genji's desire it seemed stopped at her door,
he had not claimed her, she gave thanks for that,
but he had spoken then, she heard his words:
'Let no man see you, not my son himself,
you do not know how beauty moves a man
to words he did not mean, to actions not
his own, beyond intent, and to regret,
his even more than yours.' No, she would not.
'I will not answer,' she told Kojiju,
'such notes are not for me.' 'Your Highness, that
is childish, the young man deserves at least
the courtesy of some dismissive words,
even from what I saw some pitying.
I do not know a lady who would not
have answered these sad lines, and I can think
of one who would hear happily his voice
outside her curtain speak of love's desire,
and at the last give as she would receive
the comfort of that love. Do you not think
in arms, not at arm's length, true love should be?
It is a lonely world, the lonelier
for him since you were seen, your face in dreams
his only company.' She wept, her tears
shed true since for her own like case. And still
the Princess only thought of hands, strange hands,

laid on the quiet house that was her life.
'I cannot, cannot,' she said helplessly,
'and I can say no more. Yes, tell him that.'
Kashiwagi received her answer, still
it was an answer and he chose to lay
the stress where he most wished. 'I cannot,' there
he felt she spoke her heart, she would if things
were different have let him speak his love.
Genji alone prevented and she feared.
He saw the little figure in his mind
lingering when the others fled that day,
open to life, denying her closed world.
He sorrowed for her, if it could be his
to show her what joy life could hold for her,
if through her curtains he could speak or look,
how things would change for both! And Kojiju
could not find in her heart to speak the truth.
She carried notes the Princess would not read
and she would read aloud. Nothing he said
touched where it aimed, so the sad lady as
the custom was wrote for her mistress, and
dismissively, but ever softening
with this word and with that from her own heart.
Nights she would lie and think how different
her answers would have been, her breast full bared
of all its love, till on that breast he moved
with her to love's true end that was no end
but peace attained, still to attain again.
She even visited and heard out all his love
for an unloving girl, and a strange comfort felt
in being at his bedside, holding hands
in their unhappy bond, as strange a peace
when to an unlaced breast she held his head
and felt the lips take hold, just then her child,
though to that kindness his response was tears
and soon her breast was wet with tears for two.
'If only you were she,' he said, herself
quite out of mind, only a go-between.
Now was the time for truth and she began,
his head still to her bosom to tell all.
He would not hear: 'She could not love the man,'
angry he cried, 'youth taking to its bed
an old desire! No more conceivable
than daughter taking father for her love!

She is as any other girl, like draws to like
and age to age.' 'You do not understand,'
she said, 'she fears alike both life and love.
Genji has understood, daily he comes,
his loving nights are spent with ladies who
know no such fear. For now he gentles her
as if a mare unready for its race,
but she will race as custom settles her.
Then it will seem to you just as you say,
daughter takes father to her loving arms,
youth answers old desire desirously.
In truth it will be her small price for peace
to pay him with the child he wants, not she.'
'But he has many children.' 'All too few,[4]
not as your father counts the families
his ladies yield him. No, there are such men
as ever wish to see their women breed
and think them then most beautiful, and there
are women who would ever wish to be
big by their lord,' she sighed, 'as I would wish.
That day is his far dream but he can wait,
now not a kiss lights on the lips of sleep.
Peace is the quiet home she would maintain
and love the prowler round about the house,
doors must be barred, the mistress go her rounds,
secure all things, allow no breaker-in
to reach her feelings. Life is what she fears,
one day she will escape the world a nun.'
But he would not believe. Her bosom laced,
blindly, in tears, she left an angry room.
    And now the Emperor would honour him,
the Second Princess, elder sister of
the girl who held his love should marry him,
an honour undesired. So Kojiju
came to congratulate, was held and kissed,
she came out of his unrelinquished past.
Why not the other sister? He was sad
not only for himself but for his bride.
It seemed the world was set against his love.
A while he tried affection for his wife,
found he had none, his secret passion ruled.
These days his cat was loud upon his lap,
his princess would object, he leave the room.
Sometimes he thought that Kojiju maintained

as his kind mistress might at least make life,
this new bond, bearable, but still dismissed
the thought, she was his way to where he loved.
    And yet one night he took her to his bed
and loving almost loved, but as he slept
a small sound woke him, her back turned to him
she sobbed. He took her in his arms, asked why.
She would not answer, but stroked tenderly
she said at last, 'You use me without love.'
'Love's two unfortunates,' he answered her,
'that makes a bond, my simple need of you,
it passes love. This bed, you waiting here,
will be where that need turns. Yes, I would use
you, is not pleasure's course as strong, as glad,
in you as me? And I want more, a child.
Sometimes I feel I have not long to live
and nothing of my own to leave. My own
should come from you, no woman else. My son
in you and then at suck would seem a grace
past all I hoped, and coming home to you
would be to come to love.' He loved and she
answered him joy for joy, and loving prayed,
'O Blessed One give me fruition full,
his seed make quick in me and his love grow
not once but many times.'
    Yet in the night
a thought took hold of him he could not shake,
at odds with all his words, and with the dawn
he looked at her: 'In you is all my joy,
the sweetness of your body comforting,
and from this day you are my concubine,
to bear my children, lady of my bed.
Yet I must see your princess where she lies
and silent say my farewell to a dream,
a fading dream that no more fevers me.
She is not for me now I know, but once
she maddened me and for a look, no more,
but that is life, one day it springs at you
with claws unsheathed and would tear out your heart.
One gift she gave me, you, and that mends all.
This night, it is the eve of Kamo's Feast
when men make mad with frolics in the streets
and all attendants will be gone but you
from dusk till dawn to watch the spectacle.

You can slip out and as you see me come
open a door, then flee here to your bed,
soon I will come, your arms, your body too,
will hold me safe returned and know me theirs.
A fate proceeds in this, a look began,
a look will end it all.' He was so sure,
and yet her heart misgave, her silence as
she left his arms said more than mute consent.
    Alone, he lay and thought on that request.
Why see her, why? And came self-questioning.
Things said last night and only minutes past
were meant, but then he was with Kojiju,
what would they mean when he was by himself,
defenceless against beauty so revealed,
the moon soft rising on a sable earth
to show her to perfection? He had lied
both to himself and to his last night's love,
the dream still lived, and most that sudden scene:
still the placed curtain fell, the cat still raced,
still he was staring at the lonely girl
guessing at life, and meant for him he knew.
It claimed him as the racing cat had done.
Scenes later dreamt, he would not think on them.
How the day passed he could not well have said,
but it went by and he was there at last,
the place where all his dreaming had begun.
Shunning the moonlight for the shadowed ways
he came, scarce saw the woman opening
or thought what guide was this that led him on,
the sobbing flight behind him quite unheard.
    Sounds of the night's far wantonness and play
reached even here and in her curtained bed
the Princess lightly slept. A sound more near,
a man's step in the room, brought her awake.
Genji, she thought, come to claim husband's rights
and patient she must yield, but he stayed still
and silent and conviction grew, she had
a stranger with her. If she gave no sign
of knowing he might go, and she feigned sleep,
surely a thief advantaged by this night.
Two hands came through the curtains, lifted her
as if quite weightless to their owner's breast.
She would have screamed but no sound came from her.
'So light,' he said, 'so very light, a child.

I am ashamed that it should come to this,
but since the day of the lost cat and you
revealed, a moment but enough to set
you still before my eyes, you have been mine
in every dream of you. In every dream
I have been standing here and holding you,
and asking should I do what I do next.'
She knew now who it was, but that made no
less great her fear, if anything the more.
For such as he, her sister's husband too,
to lay his hands on her, he must be mad,
and the voice was a dreamer's, as in shock
much like her own that he stood there and asked
if he should do what he would do. 'You see,'
he said, and with a gentleness that yet
more frightened her, 'I have not been myself
since that revealing day. I fell in love,
love should be happy, I was not, I had
to see you once again, hold you in arms,
these arms that till this night, save when with one
kind woman, from me hung like branches from
a lightning-stricken tree, quite dead, quite dead.'
She trembled and the trembling seemed to please,
the want of all resistance made him feel
how soft, how gentle on her love would be
when just as softly, gently, held as now.
'You must forgive me,' he went on, 'I know
I shall do all as in my dream, not I
it is that do it but the dream, and now
I find my feelings past control.' Still locked
in terror so no cry would come, she knew
herself carried into a corner of the room
where the light streamed: 'I have to make the moon
show clear your beauty as it first was seen,'
and having looked on her, 'Lovely you are
past all my dreams of you, as delicate
as blossom on the bough your lighted face,
and softer still those rosebuds that are lips,
the moonflower rich in perfume does not scent
the night air with such fragrance as your breasts
that sweat such needless fear. Why so unkind
as not to let me speak as love would speak?
Trust me, I would not, could not, ever hurt.
Men call my play upon the koto[5] sweet,

sweet, passing sweet, will be my play on you.'
    Laid on her bed and loved so tenderly
he swept her with him to such pleasuring
as left her hating, wanting, its return,
and somewhen, wanting only, in that night
fearful and wonderful found her own hands
stroking him as he loved, her lips to his,
no stranger now, drawing him to herself
as dear as she to him, her lover owned.
And all their loving done, childlike and tired
she turned into his arms and slept as if
always she had done so. The morning came
and cradled still she lay, till scarce awake
she raised her head to take the day's first kiss,
and gently he stroked down the long, long hair
past sloping hips and they made morning love.
It seemed then the most natural of ways
to start a day as yet unthought upon,
but now awareness came and side by side
they held sad hands.
    He said, 'Last night was meant,
I think in all our lives you were my love.'
'And in them all I bore you such a son,
the envy of all women,' she replied,
'life used us willing to an end not ours,
heedless what griefs might come, yet glad I was,
yes glad I was, to feel it enter me,
for I will bear your son, but never we
as father, mother, give our love to him,'
and she wept silently upon his breast.
He held her close, knew it for the last time,
already they were saying their goodbyes.
'Two figures in a dream with no regrets,
save that it ends,' he said, 'though something says
it is not all lived out. I seem to know
when I play on the koto it will be
to you I play, you answering, and I
will not play long. Outside this dream I have
nowhere to go and I am going there.'
The room was lightening, he had to leave.
They kissed, he dressed, and bent to kiss again,
from the door he looked back, it seemed at life.
When he had gone she lay and did not think,
felt only, still her naked body held

the seed of love, her hands moved over it
as had his hands, she would remember it
as now, as it was loved, soon she would dress
and life would be appearance, nothing more.
 As void of thought as she the emptiness
of early morning's streets spoke to his own,
she might make live the night again, not he,
all of its scenes he saw and all unfelt.
The image of the claws came back to him,
they did their work and the heart did not bleed,
torn out so clean nothing was left to feel.
Heartless to go, that was the heart of loss,
and he went lost both to himself and life.
He drifted home to bed and Kojiju.
Hurt thoughts and feelings met him till she saw
the lostness in his eyes and heard him say,
'Take care of me,' and no word more from him.
At once the mother-mistress moved in her,
some evil spirit had possessed his soul
or he had been bewitched in a strange bed,
the man who talked of love, a child by her,
was gone, he had to come again. She stripped
him of his clothes and in their naked bed
gathered him to her breasts as if there held
his hurt must go from him, and so he slept.
 And it was then there came the memory
of what he said, a need that passes love,
and she was needed now, his concubine;
the body had its own will free of love,
sleeping desire would wake and move on her
and life would come in her to give him life,
the final means simply a baby's cry,
for that was life itself. He had to hear!
Surely a father must forget all loss
seeing his own child at its mother's breast,
though only she could feel the little lips
and all the beauty in that answered need.
Had life begun before St Kamo's eve
or was it in the womb of time to come,
or had the Blessed One not heard her prayer?
Or heard or not she would tend where she loved.
 Keeping her rooms the Princess seemed withdrawn
into some private world, a sad recluse.
Ladies came visiting, she had to hear

their talk of Genji's mourning for the death
of Murasaki his life's one great love,
her wish before the end to take the vows
of a full nun, dissuaded from it by
affection's selfish need. She too could wish
to hear the convent's gate shut fast on her.
Some ladies might complain of lonely nights
and loveless while he mourned, but she did not.
And yet Genji himself soon left his rooms
before the days of mourning duly spent,
feeling the foolishness of all laments
for earthly loves, and sharing the night needs
his ladies felt. In one such bed he heard
of her strange state and thought of visiting.
Next day he found her more than ever shy,
she scarcely spoke. He picked a koto up
and played a tune meant for a country song,
sad, of a lover lost, and was much pleased
when she joined in and played as to herself.
It seemed a tune she knew, had played before.
That she was moved he saw, too much he thought,
what grief like his had ever come her way?
Was it the silly simple song itself
waking sad strings that he had never guessed
were there to answer in her childish heart,
for she brushed at a tear?
    Puzzled he left,
but pleased with skill that showed a practised hand,
felt touch, and an idea went with him.
These months of mourning for the ever dead
he had neglected his young wife, yes and
his other ladies too. Nights he had spent
with these for comforting, and known with them
the brief forgetting loving bodies gave,
but being many some but seldom used
and never his sad Princess. She had seemed
even for her full fifteen years naive,
a child for Murasaki's mothering
not for his love, perhaps he had been wrong.
At all events dear debts should be repaid.
It was so long since music had been heard
in his so sad establishment, but now
a concert with the koto should bring cheer
and the main hall know courtiers again.

Of course, the young Kashīwagi as best
performer should be there, the Princess play
some piece with him, his ladies all
in just such simple pretty duets joined
behind their curtains add to the sweet sound.
    Not knowing what awaited him the youth
kept to his rooms, and to his royal wife
pleaded indisposition, some sick turn
that held him from her bed, though still polite,
concerned, each time they met. His days were passed
writing, rewriting a long letter meant
for his lost love, a final memory
of that sad joyful night, all said and done.
He would himself want no memorial
if his own count of numbered days were right.
Sickness showed mortal on his face. His wife,
the court, spoke much of it and Genji heard,
but thought such challenge as the concert made
to his proved skills should bring him to himself,
for that the sickness was of mind and thence
had passed to all the vital elements
was known, the cause unknown. Yūguri came
and guessed at blighted love, at an east wind
of circumstance, but love for whom he asked.
The day of the lost cat came back to him,
but his mind shied from that and looked elsewhere,
and yet he felt his questions turned aside.
    Constant as the companion of his bed
and his day-nurse was Kojiju, her place
as concubine established, known to all.
He gave her an affection truly felt,
she asked no more. He knew he had her love
and in her arms this was a solacing
that made more dear her gift, it asked return.
He found himself wanting to give that child
he once had asked of her almost as much
as she to have it, and would sadly smile
knowing at what end all her loving aimed.
Sometimes indeed his Princess seemed a dream,
more real to him his concubine, and when
he felt that he would kiss and she would weep.
How much dependent on her he was grown
he knew, in household walks or seated hands
were never far apart, would often touch,

when they did not she guessed where his thoughts went.
    One morning he put his last letter in
her hand and patiently she took it, sought
the Princess, 'Highness, there will come no more
such missives, so the sender bids me say.'
'Is he as ill as said?' the young girl asked,
and when the messenger burst into tears,
'You love him too I see,' and they embraced.
'You share his bed I know,' the Princess said,
'you should be happy.' 'Yes, but it is you
he loves, he sickens for you. All I win
is pity for these ever open arms
that should be yours, so his sighs say. I see
him daily waste before my eyes, and all
I do is nothing, he has lost the heart
in him, the will to live.' They said no more
for Genji then came in and Kojiju
bowed and withdrew, but not before her hand
had thrust the letter under the bed quilt.
'A lady who has known unhappiness,'
the Princess said. Something had been concealed,
but his face did not alter, he talked on
about his concert and her part in it,
the best of Murasaki's pupils she
must play. He would have no excuse from her;
'This shyness would become a child, but not
a lady of your years and state and skill.
Fetch your good koto, play that air again,
that country tune that moved you so last time.
And at this concert have no needless fear,
Kashīwagi will be with you in all,
a youth who if he has a fault it is
overly to be lost in what he feels,
and he will seem to play as if from love,
and of a blemish in your play will make
an unexpected beauty. Do not fear.'
Was it his fancy that her face grew pale
and haunted eyes looked back the while he talked?
    She left for the next room, found Kojiju
who made a sign for silence, and returned.
Left to himself Genji had found his thoughts
stray to the visitor, not lovely as
men used that common word, a caring face,
it had the beauty painters tried to give

young motherhood above its child. He must
have seen her and not seen her many times
serving the Princess, so why only see
her now and see so clear? He was a fool.
The quilted bed, he scanned it, there an edge,
a missive, it went in his sleeve. Returned,
she found him still, at ease. She played, he praised,
and asked, 'Your visitor who has so much
sad beauty in her face, whom does she serve
these days?' 'The lord Kashīwagi,' she said.
'That saddens her, the beauty is her own,'
he answered. Kojiju heard all and smiled.
'And now a letter I must read,' he said,
she would soon know his meaning. But just then
relief was all she knew, at last alone
she sat and closed her eyes, then searched the bed.
Her cry brought Kojiju: 'Lost! I am lost!
He found it, he said nothing, reads it now.'
    And the two women stared at unformed thoughts,
fearful in speculation, of the two
the Princess least herself. Almost a child
the other thought, an age to dream upon,
not bear love's weight as she had borne his love,
drained his full soul. She had to think for her:
'Your Highness, you must do away with fear,
show none, say nothing the next time he calls.
You will find he says nothing too. Of course,
he will think much, but the chief sufferer
could be your lover, and he suffers now.
What would this do to him? He has to hear
only of sad farewell. Genji will think
of the disgrace to you, your sister and
your lover's father, not least to himself.
He will remember how a curtain fell
and showed you to a love past all control,
this love that rapes us all, the rapist held
so dear in arms. Oh he will understand,
and you have peace, he will not use your bed.
And when you meet, show him a face that says,
"What use to speak of sad things that have been?"
Do I talk sense?' The Princes hoped she did,
and Genji having thought knew that she did.
Besides, he had his concert to prepare
and he would not have this news hindering.

Yet love's rape brought one unwished consequence,
not her conception forcing a wry smile,
for babies could not be unwished by him,
not even this one, but through pleasured nights
still he must suffer silently in beds
he visited congratulations on
his fathering, and at his age, a child,
and know his ladies hoped like happiness,
their wishful arms somehow more urgent felt;
he could accept their all-unknowing words
yet with the morning they came back to taunt.
Yes, he could suffer all and as he did
think on his brief sight of the visitor
with haunting face, and on Kashīwagi
in that east wind of circumstance his own
good son had guessed too well, a misplaced love.
And still the lad must not hear of his child.
But someone did, Kojiju visited.
She had her own news, she too had conceived
and near the night the Princess had. She had
to talk: 'He was so happy, loving, free
of his sick lethargy, he laughed, almost
you would have thought he wanted me that night
to have conceived again, talked nonsense of
a beauty new to me, had to feel where
his own child grew, and then said something strange,
"His brother should be growing now, they will
meet on one breast", but he was mad, quite mad
in joy of love.' She sobered, 'But with dawn
an invalid lay at my side, all that
brief brightening quite gone, and yet I hope.'
The Princess said, 'We knew the night we loved,
how neither knows, that I would bear a son.
I too conceived, we both carry his child,
but it is you alone will bear his hope,
see him with it in arms to smile on it
if prophecies should fail, as pray they will,
for he can never claim his son by me.
Our night was not a dream without regrets.'
'And yet I envy you that dream. I am
the concubine in whom his needs are met,
who for affection gives unanswered love
and now a baby his arms may not hold.'
'If that should happen then there will be two

that leave this life, for I must ask what you
will think unnatural. When I give birth
your breasts, not mine, will suckle my own child.
The convent's gates will shut on me, it has
some time been my desire, and since love came
and went in the one night it has grown firm.
I know that Genji will respect my wish,
you would come here and all be in his care.
He may love women, he loves children more.
May your loss never come, but if it does
will you do as I ask, take him? I want
the two to grow as brothers, feel for you
as mother.' Silence grew, after a time
was broken, Kojiju said simply, 'If
what most I fear should come, then we will talk,'
and thought, 'Still I am made the go-between.'
    The court spoke more and more of his strange state.
His father, who had many children and
by many ladies, came and showed delight
in Kojiju's plain pregnancy. The glow
of health mantled her face, a beauty not
so evident before, her belly gave
a dignity he thought, she was as she
should be, as any loving woman should.
A pity that the princess his son's wife
stayed barren. But this gifted son of his,
yes the most gifted of his many sons,
diverse of qualities, to come to this!
No seeming love of woman or career,
a lonely interest in nature's face
of grass and trees and flowers, yes insects too,
and above all the music he could make
as no one else, a dreamer and withal
a football player of surpassing skill,
the single trait from father passed to son,
was it these qualities despite black moods
that made him loved by Genji, Yūguri,
and even brought him to a royal match?
One more surprise, that this young concubine
big with his seed had proved his husbandry.
He smiled on her leading him to his son,
but did not smile when brought into his room.
    'My lord has been most sick,' said Kojiju,
'and more than partner of his bed I am

his nurse.' And she would nurse him more than well,
in bed and out, the father thought, and much
he needed her, the lad was ill, of what?
It was as if the life were out of him.
Seeming to read his father's mind the youth
had risen smiling, 'This will pass,' he said,
'one of those things,' but his eyes did not smile
and their gaze went in search of Kojiju.
'Sit down,' the order came, 'prayers must be said,
not that I have much faith in prayer, your nurse
is more your need. Do as she says.' 'It seems
more of the mind than body sir,' she said,
'he should get out, see persons, things, he liked.'
'A good advice, take it, most practical.
I want no more of this,' he brusquely said,
but fear was in his voice. 'Yūguri best
of friends will call again, and Genji asks
for your assistance. He would have you play
in a grand concert to be held, he says,
in Murasaki's memory. She loved
the simple koto of our land, its tunes
all country airs to songs our mothers sang.
You will play to a courtly audience,
a lady your unseen accompanist,
and he asks for your pretty concubine.
The Emperor regrets he cannot come
but, his First Minister, I shall be there.
Genji thinks music, company, will rouse
your failing spirits, make you man again.'
    Surely the nurse agreed with that he thought,
and was surprised to hear her quick dissent,
'My lord, this is not what I meant, it is
too sudden, taxing, the lord Genji will
not take offence if he move quiet, step
by step, back into company.' But now
it was Kashīwagi who spoke: 'Forgive
my lady, father, I will go. There had
to be a time. I owe him a great debt
and this is but the slightest of returns,
long due.' The father looked between the two,
what debt beyond small kindnesses he could
not guess, they scarce weighed his son's health, and yet
this was the wanting spirit, a good sign,
women were born to nurse and if indulged

made children of their men. Best leave alone,
let them decide. He saw the concubine
had turned away in tears, strangely unsure
he looked at both and left.
    Kashīwagi
now held his lady close, kissed her wet eyes,
'My little mother,' he said softly, 'I
think you know well my debt.' 'Yes, and it is
paid in the dearest kind.' He questioned her
by look but she went on: 'Some debts are past
all payment, yours is not. Lord Genji is
most kind, thinks of your love, your father, and
even he thinks of you. This kindness he
learned in the heats of youth, a boy he took
his father's wife, young and too beautiful
and more than willing in her curtained bed,
it haunts him still, he pays in the one coin,
remorse. The emperor is his own son.
So the talk goes. A convent has her, there
she will receive your lady, understand.'
A while there was a silence, then he said,
'None of it was my doing, all was dreamt,'
and she, 'There speaks the voice that most I dread.
It is not any debt to him that moves your mind,
but something like the sense of a path made
for you to walk, each step foretold, the end
of that path death. Say I imagine all
but in your loving fit the night I spoke
of my conception strange things then were said,
my widowed breasts were to feed one more child.
Do you deny it? If there were a debt
it would be nearer home. Shall I give birth
in sorrow, know you dead, and your son grow
more like you every day in dearest ways
still to be grief's reminder? This is what
you want?' 'No, but I have no choice in this,
nor Genji, though he thinks he has, has choice
of my accompanist. Say that I could
elect another way if I so willed
the end would be the same. You have guessed well.
Love me what time remains is all I ask,
for saddest thing of all you will forget
me, happy as if I had never been.
No, no protest, for now I have your love,

and wish that in my all-controlling dream
my love had gone to you, but it did not.'
And nothing further would he say to her,
but come the night he loved as if all life
were in her and he should not love again,
and she as if the parting spirit stayed
only that while she held him and he loved.
One thing he promised, she would hear him play
and his strength would not fail the while he played.
   The concert came, Genji sat in mid-hall,
musicians and then courtiers about,
beyond these all his ladies, curtained but
still able to see through their slitted screens,
some there prepared to play, the Princess one,
her face set not to show emotion and
never to smile, in hand her instrument
ready to lift at the so dreaded cue,
all as foreseen, his play, her answering,
and would he not play long? Had lady Death
curtained herself from him this waiting while
to play tonight? A fancy out of tune
with that bright scene, not with Kashīwagi,
for opposite she saw the fine-honed face,
the spirit shining like a naked light
from its spare tegument of skin and bone.
Beside her sat his concubine, gaze fixed
upon the stillness that yet spoke leashed power,
unleashed last night with such a force she cried
for joy, yet had to ask what that force meant.
Once they saw Genji come and question him
and his head merely nod, and hesitant
Genji return to his director's seat,
still glancing at him and unhappily.
   Kashīwagi at peace in inner space
knew this was where he had to come, the time,
and quiet heard what he would play, the tune
so simply called 'Farewell', though that did not
say all that he would say, knew what the night
held for two women. For his own rapt self
the end to which he played was everything.
Buddha, but he was tired, his piece the last!
Someone had finished and now Genji's fan
pointed at him. He closed his eyes and played.
So gentle, low and pleading his first sounds

she could not miss the way she was to go,
and she came in uncertain, pleading too,
he had to understand, love had no say
where it would light, your bed was made for you.
And now his pace was fast, his pitch was high,
was felt as desperate, how could he live
without her loveliness? And from a height
he fell to a sweet run of notes, so ran
his feelings in their days of love. Came in
her touch with all decision sad, last notes
heard each one yet more faint, retreating steps,
steps of relinquished love. He struck one chord
and on the silence it fell like a sob.
And there all should have ended, he played on,
a flourish of defiance, there was love
still in the world and love to answer it,
and if not in this world in worlds beyond.
He stopped, his instrument fell to his side,
a strangely silent hall erupted then,
men stood applauding, Genji standing too.

The player stayed quite still, he did not bow,
slowly bent to one side and moveless lay.
A cry rang through the hall, a woman's cry.
Genji was with him now and tearing at
collar and vest and vainly listening
at the still heart. He rose: 'Kashīwagi
our friend is gone, gone with the music fetched
out of that other life where most he lived.
I brought him to the koto one more time,
it was his last, and at my erring wish.
I know that the wise mother of his child,
perhaps another too, will not forgive,
but of his father here who has to feel
with her I ask forgiveness as a friend.'
'Genji, the will in him to live was spent,
his wish was to be here and make an end,
and well he ended. Nothing to forgive,
the tears that are in my eyes are in yours.
Yuguri, you will see your friend brought home,
his lady with him, the rest is for me.'
Men stood in talking groups, Genji's voice rang,
'Friends, go your ways, the concert is at end.'
Alone in the great hall he sat and thought
of nothing else but that last flourish, what

was meant by it when by a dying man
so lively played, still there was life, still love.
How could there be? And yet it had felt right
while music played that seemed to find the soul.
Silence might fall on a tune sounding still.
    Months later when the Princess bore her child
she turned away and asked for Kojiju,
'My time is come,' she said, 'take him. This life
that killed Kashīwagi is not for me,
the child would bind me to it. I will wait
it out in convent walls. In other lives
I know that we will meet, I be his love,
though neither as you knew us in this world,
and in them all loving conceive by him,
not in the stolen sweetness of a night
but in the way of husband with his wife,
lover with mistress, as the time decides.'
Nothing that they could say would move her mind,
it seemed that nature's voice in her was stilled
and something not of this world spoke in her.
She only said, 'He would have wanted it'.
So the child newborn went to Kojiju
and to the breast where one more child had been.
    She lived in the room Genji had assigned
and silent there he often came and watched
her suckle both the children at her breasts,
as silent left. His visits came to be
expected. One day when she smiled he thought
her smile above the babies beautiful
as no smile he had seen, its tenderness
touching the infinite, the appetites
of two small beings put to sleep on such
soft beds and rich he had to envy them.
That night he came, as she had wished he would,
and lay with her and peace filled all the room.
'An old desire' Kashīwagi had said,
but all she knew was reassuring arms,
he would be father, she the mother, of
another's sons. One cried, she left his side
to suckle it, he watched it feed and shared
in its content.
    With him again she said,
'I am a simple woman with one need,
still to be needed.' 'And you are,' he said.

'I thought that love had done with me and left
only a due affection. So it was
with Murasaki whom I mourned, custom
had long outlived what surely must have been
and left observance only. Nights I spent
with one or other of my ladies were
no more than payment for adventures past
and kindnesses received, so sentiment
gathers them in their need beneath one roof,
but with them I am still alone. And now
the stranger to my life that changes all
is come, my feelings say I am in love.
My eyes seek out your eyes, dwell on your face,
my hands would touch you and not know to stop,
I see you walk and wish my child in you.'
'Love me, my lord,' she said, and she was loved
into a night felt full of promises.
She slept and woke: 'A man Kashīwagi,
a princess too, together went away
and left me two fine boys to love, and you,
it was a dream.' 'It was a dream,' he said.

Notes:

1 This story is a much altered version of an episode in **The Tale of Genji** by Murasaki Shikibu, c. 1020. The main change is in the leading role given to Kojiju, a minor figure in the Tale. Japanese vowels are as in Italian. I use the stroke above for stress, though Japanese has no stressed vowels.

2 Murasaki Shikibu mentions a game of football at this point.

3 Once owned a woman could only be seen by her owner.

4 The early polygamy of wealthy or noble Japanese has to be remembered.

5 A three-stringed or seven-stringed instrument native to Japan.

OUTCAST LOVE

Face it, we are all fools, folk thought and felt
as the tale tells, so hard to be or man
or woman and no more, as nature meant.
The cobbler seated on Adzuma Bridge
heard the known step and as it halted bowed.
Said the lord Takoji, a handsome youth
of five and twenty years, 'Duties await
me on the Castle hill, I cannot go[1]
with sandal thong thus broken, see to it,'
and as the cobbler worked, 'Always you bow
and always stirs and goes from me some lost
or sleeping memory.' 'Would that my own
so slept,' came the reply. 'A boy I helped
trim your late father's lawns, clear the quick streams,
calm lakes, where once he found his peace. Amid
his trees and flowers I walked in happiness,
with you I ran the Hatamoto lands.
It was my dream to be a gardener.
Innocence had its dream and both were lost,
for grown I haunted women, came to this.
'Now I am made unclean, by need reduced[2]
to this pariah trade, to leather work,
at least no butcher of the beast men chase
or breed. For is not life a holy thing
in its wild movements as its tame? Nor am
I fallen to an executioner.
Buddha has spoken, for his saying all
that do these works, yes and their womenfolk,
pollute the house of man. Unclean by birth
or by our trades unclean, kept to our clan
and quarter, only free in our day-work.
My chief here is Kihachi, a good man.'
'I had not thought on this,' said Takoji,
'difference I was born to, it seemed life,
nor thought on you. Forgive me, now I know
you for that Chokichi who played with me,
brightened the sad hours of a lonely boy,
I think the only friend he ever knew.
Children will change, forget old selves, old friends.
Here, take these riyos, all the help on me.
They did not think life holy who could kill
my father. No priest's voice condemned that war,

it was but kill and kill.' The cobbler smiled,
'This world that fears my shadow cast on it
is not for feeling, and you always felt.'
    But as they spoke along the bridge there came
two singing-girls and stood regarding them.
One might have been some twenty years or so,
the other fifteen, little more, but far
the lovelier it seemed to Takoji,
the other comely, this one beautiful,
her body budding to its season's flower.
The innocence of maidenhood was in
the gaze that met and did not meet his own.
He saw dark hair so brilliant in the sun
it had the sheen of blue. She shone for him.
The eyes long lashed were rush-fringed lakes so clear.
Everything of her seen was delicate,
such promise spoke from the soft parted lips
drawn as with finest brush-stroke a rose-red,
delicate the small breasts, waist slim, hips slight.
What shape of beauty would be hers to show
her bright kimono gone![3] Her instrument
doubtless shed music from its fine-tuned strings
but none like that the singing air must hold
when she shed all her clothes, or even now
he heard in her shy smile. He fell in love.
Seeing such looks exchanged the elder girl
seized her friend's hand and drew her whence they came,
but not without the younger looking back.
    'Who were these maidens?' then asked Takoji.
'They are my O Kuma who comes for me,
the young girl our chief's daughter O Koyo.
No tongue but speaks her praise. Yet outcast both
why does your honour ask?' 'You were my friend,
you are my friend, will you do as I say?'
'As a friend should.' 'Then bring the girl to me.
I want her with such wanting as but once
in a life comes and then becomes that life.
Friend, do you dream, for even now I dreamt
and yet I was broad waking. There she went,
the figure of my dream, and as she went
she looked to me and I knew it no dream,
and she was mine. Bring her to me and soon!'
'My lord, you do not know the thing you ask,
one of her kind your woman! If word got

to the High Governor the honoured name
of Hatamoto would be blotted out,
lands lost, yourself become an exile far
among the hills, a peasant in rude fields,
and for one such! Think, think again, my lord.'
'Think, think!', cried Takoji, 'I will not think,
but how I feel I know, as in my life
never. I want her for my woman, love,
my anything! Speak to her father, lay
on him the charge.' And he was gone.
The cobbler sat unhappy: 'What use words?
I can but watch and ward, see how things go.
Perhaps discreetly done all may go well,
a little passing hurt to O Koyo,
this passion overblown a lesson learned,
and as he says her father bears the charge.
Yet all will fall on me and O Kuma,
for they are children and most Takoji
who risks so much.' That day he saw the chief,
'The Hatamoto seeks a concubine
and he would have your daughter.' He was heard
in silence, the chief used to judgments on
the problems of his people now must weigh
one nearer home. Danger was here, but there
was honour, she would mount a noble bed
once her lord knew his need of her, himself
have noble grandsons. He was loath to lose
the brightness of her presence, she had come
so late in life, and with her mother's death.
A moment he saw the same fate for her,
shut his eyes to it, she must take her chance.
Her days would be more fair, her birth unknown
a fiction might bring her to marriage-bed,
and even as a concubine her lord
must love the get of his own loins, provide
for them. And then his people, fancy swayed,
change had to come, and it might come in bed
and with his O Koyo. His mind made up
he looked at Chokichi: 'See that they meet
outside of Honjo. You, your O Kuma,
I want you to be with them, keep things safe.'
The couple met in one of two fair rooms
upstairs in Oji teahouse.[4] Separate
they went. Her friend soon left her for the arms

of Chokichi, and the shy O Koyo
stayed feeling eyes on her she could not meet.
There was a bed, against one wall a bench,
and there still and untouching the girl sat
and nothing saw, only his presence felt.
Beside her Takoji, whose wishful gaze
moved ever on her face as if compelled,
said suddenly, 'I see you in the nights
and there you lie my loved and loving wife.'
It was as if a world within went still,
then she was in his arms and crying 'No!
That cannot be, your sweetheart, not your wife,'
half weeping and all happy just to know
that he could feel that way, and he surprised
by his own words, that he could mean them too.
And now embraced his lips found out her neck
and dreamt on it with kisses still renewed,
and on her lips, and there their loving ceased
save that, her head laid quiet to his breast,
silent the two looked into happy space.
And Chokichi so finding them was not
ill pleased, nor O Kuma who with a kiss
welcomed her to the sisterhood of love.

From that day the pair never failed to meet,
but now passion roved free and on the bed
she waited for its instant covering,
open to him she gave herself to joy.
'I did not live till now,' he said. 'Nor I,'
and far away heard herself moan and cry.
And so, left to themselves and a locked room
desire was grown a fierce and naked thing,
she was indeed the loveliness he dreamt,
and having him she knew his taken love
a wonder and delight, while taking her
he knew he gave his soul as she gave hers
and both had given since that first fond sight.
He was her lord, simply she saw it so,
and he could say, 'You own me, and our love
has ceremony in the act itself,
we are made man and wife.' And now the word
brought no protest, was heard as natural.
Indeed they were love's innocents, the world
made to the fashion of their wishfulness.

But now not O Kuma beside him could

calm the more troubled thought of Chokichi,
and some part his concern was shared by her.
They were both of a kind, their loves enjoyed
challenged no state of things, no custom kept,
except their being where they should not be,
the other two were different. Despite
his first misgivings never had he dreamt,
conceived, the chance that Takoji would feel,
as any eyes could see, so strongly for
his outcast love, tradition made a tale,
known consequence a fable, all that he
had told him on Adzuma Bridge unheard,
his bridge to ruin Chokichi now saw.
This was no manageable love affair,
discretion had no part in it, there was
a dreadful innocence in this mad love.
O Kuma's hand sought his, she felt the same,
and she feared too this thing would turn on them.
    One afternoon, the door unlocked, they found
a fondling pair, naked, oblivious
of presence, and when noticed seemingly
quite careless of their state. Slowly they dressed,
shut in their private world as slowly kissed
when Takoji went off alone. A space,
and O Koyo her eyes quite blind and yet
seeing her lover and his lips on her
went with her friends, and if O Kuma spoke
she was not heard. Chokichi thought and thought,
he was to 'keep things safe', but how to check
a love so wild before great hurt befall?
Hurt either way and yet he had to act,
and how to move the father to such hurt?
A plain tale would not do, a lie must serve.
    That night he saw the chieftain, 'Sir,' he said,
'word has gone to the councillors most close
to Hatamoto, how I do not know,
of this affair, their fear of our loathed race,
our touch, warns what must come if he pursue
this passion. He has listened, thought on it,
and though with a protesting and sore heart
bows to the urgent will of family.
They must keep silence, but you surely see
what end this outlaw love must have for him.
I rue the day I heeded his desire

and for your daughter's sake.' 'And you, as he,
are right,' sadly the chief replied. 'You did
as asked, I listened much too readily.
And now she loves him?' 'Never have I seen
such love. So owned by it, they are as one
in its enchantment, not to be unspelled.
Yes she is sick in love, as he, and grief
will be their portion many days. What else?
Yet we must keep these stricken loves apart
and if he weakens say that she is ill.
Time may make dull the hurt, though not remove.'
'You do not know her well,' the father sighed.
O Koyo took to bed, left food and drink,
pined for her lord. Still she lay in his arms,
no part of her young body but his lips
yet pressed, and as a husband takes his wife
she had been taken, she could not forget.
It was so simple, why could he not have
what was his own, her wholly given self?
That he felt as before and loved her still
she knew, and felt the parting pain no less
this too she knew, but it did not console.
Times there were when she dreamt of such love made
as passed beyond its action to a state
where nothing stayed their loving, made it stop,
and waking wept on the same loveless bed.
O Kuma visiting would leave in tears,
seek comfort of her lover, sad as she,
his 'necessary lie' but half believed.
To Takoji quite lost and questioning
the cobbler spoke of illness, illness, some
sore fever keeping her confined, and his
advice, 'Forget all this, one of our kind
is not for you,' said nothing to his heart.
What she had given him was love entire,
love he had never known, no more than she.
A month or more of his unhappiness
had passed when thoughts of joy disused
took him to Oji and the scene he knew,
so still by day, now with the night so loud
with talk and laughter that from the dark street
he listened more alone. Girls there were here,
none O Koyo. A voice spoke from the door:
'My lord, is all remembrance gone? Sazen,

once ronin,[5] in your father's retinue,
now sunk to fortune-teller still I make
a modest living. But this common haunt
is not for you.' 'Agreed,' said Takoji,
thinking how one room so uncommon was
when he and O Koyo loved there, and that
this fellow Sazen fitted with the night,
his features had convenience writ on them,
the quick eyes looked for opportunity.

A moment's thought and the decision made,
'I need advice and you might be the man
to give it.' 'Willingly,' the other said,
'if you will step this way to my mean place.'
Across a table Sazen heard enough,
said the expected things of misplaced love,
and then, 'Still there is something strange in this,
one day a healthy loving girl, the next
reported illness and no word from her,
almost it seems these people shut her from
your knowledge for their good - or for your own?
You say your playmate Chokichi had charge.'
And on that last word paused, 'Leave this to me.'
They parted, the brisk fortune-teller for
Honjo, the outcast quarter. In the street
lord Takoji considered: 'A mad world!
What sickness in its faiths, its fantasies!
Pollution from my love, it goes beyond
conception, the fine flower the garden yields
might just as well be deemed a poison-weed.
This rogue I use polluted, yes, not she!
Let them cite custom, I will go my way
that is the way of nature, and to her.'

Come to his hateful goal, 'What's in a name?',
the ronin said, 'Call these folk what you will,
they are for use, one will be used tonight',
and found his way to the chief's house and room.
'They tell me that your daughter sickens here.
I as a fortune-teller without sight
of the sad patient can say now she mends
quite soon, and I would add, lord Takoji
asks after her most tenderly. Silence
about her state, no word from her, he does
not understand.' 'Nor do I understand,'
the chief said, 'Chokichi made it quite clear,

the Hatamoto family forbids
all interest, and the young man accedes.'
'Then I must say that Chokichi has lied,
perhaps for reasons he thought good. A child
he played with my good lord, met him again.
Made what he is, not born, he may have wished
to keep untouched by stain his Takoji.
And yet what stain can be in loveliness
so dearly praised? My lord finds none and sighs.'
This Sazen said, his mercenary soul
set on a gainful service with no thought
for whom he served, and knowing well his words
reached the fond father's heart of love and pride,
hope even for his folk untouchable!
'At once my daughter has to hear of this,
it will put colour in her cheeks this month
not seen, restore lost appetite. But that
our Chokichi should lie, who would have thought.'
The ronin idly shrugged, well he had read
this Chokichi and hence the truth of things.
The chief would have been gone, but Sazen stayed
his hasty steps: 'A moment, my good sir,
nothing said to the cobbler, O Kuma
keep from the sickroom, most important, wait
my note with all instructions. Understood?'
A nod received, Sazen went off well pleased,
glad to be out of tainted company,
and money, so it seemed upon his way
scenting the evening air. Still less than had
the cobbler on Adzuma Bridge did he
conceive of more than an affair in this,
nor had he prescience of harm to come
as O Kuma. The letter went next day.
O Koyo brightened like a springtime dawn,
away her winter's night, her path was strewn
with sunshine flowers, hope shone, once more she lay
in Takoji's fond arms. Her maiden years,
all inexperience till he had come,
prepared her for love's table as the scene
nature had meant for her, where she would know
only the happiness of serving him,
no harm come in, once she was there, to vex.
That such had come and gone meant only this,
always the master sun broke through undimmed.

One tenet of her faith she kept quite clear,
she was made for his use, the use of love.
What else she was or did weighed not at all.
    Next day the note, Kihachi read with care,
grief for lost O Koyo and sour distaste
for one task put on him, he must enact
a fiction that would pain both Chokichi
and O Kuma, and all for the new life
and love of O Koyo with Takoji.
Yet she was no more his but in her heart
belonged to her own man, and he must help.
The way to Oji was dispiriting
as no way he had known, while she could smile
about her on a land of promises,
and still she understood and pressed his hand
to show she too felt the goodbye to come.
At Sazen's door he kissed her and was gone.
Almost a mother he had been, her room
would stay untouched where he so often had
looked in to see she slept. Only his feet
found the way back to Honjo and to home.
To her knock the door opened near at once.
She was sent up a stair to a small room
with bed, table and seat. Sazen had kept
his distance on the stair and here. He said,
'When I bring food wait on that bed, and when
I clear the table be there too,' and went.
A strange man and she felt so much alone,
many a tune she played upon the strings
and sang to them and waited on love's step.
    Come home, as much alone, the chief thought on
his second task, almost as much disliked
but vital to all else, his lying tale.
This fellow Sazen smooth of tongue, he should
have told it. No, it had to come from him.
He went pretending tears, not all pretence,
to where the cobbler lived with O Kuma.
She was not there, but Chokichi received
him, sat him down and waited painfully.
His guest seemed overcome, words lost, and then:
'Good master, what a grief is fallen here,
O Koyo drowned! She could not bear love's loss,
like a hand slipping from its hold at sea
let loose her life. Hopeless she pined away,

would see no one at last, not O Kuma.
In her sick night mindless she must have walked
down to that rapid river and to death,
washed to what lengths and depths of darkness who
shall say, and all for love first given, then
withdrawn. I cannot blame myself enough
for letting her so love. My daughter gone!'
Dazed, staring, Chokichi heard all, sat dumb.
'You blame yourself!', at last he cried. 'I curse
myself, I started what too late I stopped,
and now her image will swirl through my mind
each time I look down from Adzuma Bridge
on that death's water.' Troubled by that cry,
confused, moved to some gesture of amends,
untimely the chief tried to press on him
a purse of money, and then wordless left.
    Bitter against himself the cobbler paced.
A master cobbler, he had cobbled death!
If O Kuma were here! Twice he had passed
a piece of parchment where the chief had sat,
doubtless drawn from a pocket with that purse
so strangely offered, now picked up, spread out
a note. A glance stopped on his name, he read
and all came clear. He laughed, a puppet-play,
this Sazen deadly master at the strings,
all was pretence, their motives differing,
his own lie had put all in Sazen's hands,
his greedy trustless hands. Well, he would pay.
O Koyo and her Takoji, they loved
and did not think, the world would seek them out.
The old man, his beloved daughter ill,
was easy prey. But Takoji in love
most troubled him, one simple lover's slip
and the affair was out, the judgment sure
on all. One last appeal, should it be made?
    The door flew open and his O Kuma
was in his arms and crying: 'Oh my love,
what have we done? Our O Koyo is gone!
The chief says lost in that dread river where
so many go, this for a path that led
from her own door and sometimes she would walk,
among wildflowers she loved, right to the brink.
Or could she wander now the ways, witless,
alone and sad?' The anger grew in him,

he read aloud the letter. Listening
tears changed to smiles, 'So she is safe and in
her Takoji's kind arms.' She could not think
past the relief she felt. 'All's well,' she said,
'no need to cry for her. My Chokichi,
love me as she is loved, to the same height
of happiness, the same forgetfulness.'
Things were not at an end, but she lay still
in given peace, his lips clasped to a breast,
and when he said, 'I love you O Kuma,'
'Hush baby,' she replied, 'such needless words.'
She had not understood and Takoji
was not her care. Just then he seemed so far
removed from her. A sadness touched his kiss,
'Something I have to do, or try to do.'
Dusk was nearhand she thought, he would be back
to wake her to his love, smiling she slept.
    Just then in Sazen's room the lovers met.
O Koyo's eyes were bright with yearning and
his heart beat fast. She felt his seeking hands,
and trembled to their touch as will a foal
that feels along its flanks slow, steadying,
its master's stroke, delighting as it moves.
Her eyes closed to the kiss upon her neck
claiming, reclaiming all, and all was his.
Some talk there was of past unhappiness,
but soon they were in bed and all griefs gone,
their joys more sharp for the remembered pain,
body to body never quite so dear.
A moment still, 'This man who houses me
keeps a strange distance. Out of fear of you?'
'Not that, my innocent,' he said. 'Forget
him, soon I will search out a country house
where you are mistress and I visit you,
and at such times we will be happy as
no two have been, living and loving one.'
    'My lord,' sometime she asked, 'why should a girl
so young find favour in your eyes?' He thought:
'I have loved beauty as it touched my heart
and that was with its promise, in the bud.
The rose full blown, it has no more to say,
the budding rose can set a man to dream
of days to be, so in young eyes, young lips,
the dawning loveliness that is your smile,

the ripening, not ripeness, of your breasts,
I see what love has still to offer me.
Oh you are Spring itself with flowers to grow.
You are all promise and such promise as
still grows with giving. Still I see the girl,
lips parted on a smile, that one bright morn
stood shedding music on Adzuma Bridge.'
    'Love is a wonder that it comes at all,
could we have thought in this great crowded world
we should find one another for our love?
When you possess me, take me from myself,
why then I am in heaven a soul blest,
above this earth where there's nor you nor me
but as it were a thing celestial.'
His answer was to love her and confirm
all she had said of something beyond self
that took possession, reached another world.
Once there she cried, now back with him he said,
'You could not dream any but blessed dreams,
others have had bad dreams but never you,
yet we must speak of these, they threaten us.
    'In theirs men bind and sever, to their will
turn nature from its kindly course and use.
You are defilement to their sick-cast thought,
no woman but a thing untouchable,
and loving you is sacrilege to them.
They menace with the hurt of severance,
so we grow liars, and good friends for us.
Now you shed tears,' 'Tears for us all,' she said.
'Nothing in this was simple as I thought.
It seemed so natural for me to love.
The how and why I did not think, it was.
Still to be giving, still be taken, if
it could be so!' 'It can,' he reassured,
'Still I would find you, for, let the worst come,
let the great Hatamoto name be lost,
that were no fault of mine but of bad dreams.
Oh I am mad in love, my O Koyo,
and with no will to mend, but know that I
talk sense as love has taught, the best of sense.'
    'An outcast born I never thought of it.
Even when once good O Kuma brought home
a wounded woman from the street that else[6]
had lain to die, one of our kind, to me

it was a day's event, next day forgot.
And there was pride, father would say, "Our men
know many skills, a Samurai his sword."
So cosseted by father, friends, their love,
my life and all in it was marvellous
and I accepted it just as it came.
And even now it is as if I had
expected you, always the marvellous.
And the new wonder wakes in me a wish,
a craving more, that has in it some fear,
remembering my mother so like me,
and how she died, in this young womb to bear
your given child and press it past my pains,
your hand held tight by mine, into the light,
its father's son.' Wordless he kissed, and then:
'One day in all my life means everything,
when distances of all kinds were denied
and had no being, so love lived in us.
Come good, come ill, we were made one that day.'
    But as they spoke boldly to Sazen's door
came Chokichi, and opened elbowed in.
If he had known! And yet he had to speak.
Who this would be Sazen could guess at once,
'Cobbler, get out of here!' the ronin cried,
'Your loathly kind pollutes the meanest house.'
'Then you will not want the girl O Koyo.'
That fool Kihachi! Sazen changed his tune,
'These thirty riyos, take them and be gone.'
The sum would never serve, Sazen in fear,
finding his gainful role as love's good host
more risk than gain was Chokichi's one aim.
He said, 'A hundred riyos at the least
to buy my silence,' and with the demand
knew his life put in peril, for the man
would never think that for the lovers' sakes
no word would have been spoken. Friend as boy
but now a needy cobbler, he would see
in him the bold blackmailer, dangerous.
As Sazen did, 'That money is not here,
but at the Hatamoto residence
I can secure it in his honour's name.'
    Chokichi thought, 'I walk with death, but I
am set. Watchful I go along, take and
return it, honesty should lend its voice

and Takoji listen for the last time,
make his unhappy choice, I guess which one
but then I will have played my part.' A nod,
the ronin felt the knife sharp by his side.
The two were wary as they took the road,
their way deserted in the fallen dusk
and soon far from the central haunts of men,
Sazen still waiting vantage that escaped
him yet, when suddenly upon a stone
Chokichi stumbled and the knife went in,
not once but thrice. Casting a quick look round
he saw no one had seen and hurried home,
washed from his blade the blood. His guests loved on,
oblivious as O Kuma in sleep.
'They will pay dear for their night's play,' he vowed.
Payment was made but not as he had meant.
    The Wardsman's men making their daily round
found the dead body, on it was a note.
One of the tainted caste so found would not,
as custom viewed such deaths, have merited
a further search and action, but the note
had names to interest, report was made,
the last thing that the dead man could have wished.
Put to the question Sazen soon confessed.
Sentence was passed in the great Castle Hall,
the four accused laden with diverse cares,
the chief and Takoji for O Koyo
who tried to smile for them and sadly failed,
Sazen grim-lipped, seeing too clear his fate,
and all their thoughts turning on Chokichi.
    That night they were to spend in Castle cells,
with morning sentence to be carried out:
Sazen to execution by the rite
of the three spears cast by an unclean hand;[7]
to the high Chief of all their kind for doom
O Koyo and her father, doubly then outcast,
from the untainted and from their own folk;
on all the Hatamotos loss of name
and lands, their head polluted brought on all
his kin the like pollution, Takoji
himself to a far banishment. He thought,
where superstition rules unreason is
both Chief and Governor, its madness theirs.
    Sometime he paid a guard to carry word

to the High Governor, if only for
his father's memory who had been friend,
asking permission to see O Koyo.
Permission came, he was led to her cell
where they embraced: 'Remember, love, still wait
for me, however long my search, still think
your hand in mine as it will be one day.'
'I cry for O Kuma,' she said, 'so much
alone. And this I should not think, but now
to part in such a place of gloom darkens
all thought, I am not strong, if on the ways
I die look after her. And the same thing,
we had our night, so often I was loved!
You know my fear, how would I be out there?'
'Only one night, so many other times
and then no child conceived. No, it will wait
until I come,' he said, 'and O Kuma
will be with you all ways you go. Trust me.
Out in the sun, away from this sad place,
you will be as you were. But my guard signs.
I love you O Koyo. For the last time
wait for me, I will come.' They kissed,
he went, learned from the guard the Castle gates
were haunted by a woman asking for
his O Koyo. 'That will be O Kuma,'
he said, 'tell her, "At Asakusa wait".'
'How could you do it, sir?' the guard asked once.
'Love,' answered Takoji, 'for love, for love.'
The morning came, they went their diverse ways,
Sazen's the shortest. They were made to watch.
The human thing that jerked so wild, with all
three casts at last was still. In Takoji
died then respect for justice, cruelty
was in its sentencing, no end was served.
O Koyo stood with eyes shut fast but heard.
And it was then that Takoji first felt
to leave the Castle, and the world that thought
it needed it, was to leave death for life.
Where the old man would go he could not guess
but far from towns and his own quartered folk.
So the two lovers wandered in the hills
and Takoji never gave up pursuit
of his life's love. He would do hillsman's work,
ask for an old man and young girl with friend,

always in vain, yet on the ways her face
beckoned him on, winds brought to him her voice.
In fields past the soon understanding smiles
of women he would see his O Koyo.
And he was changed, title, estate, well lost,
he was himself, welcomed by other men,
given his part in all their many tasks,
sharing their working meals and offered roofs.
So passed the unavailing years, and yet
not unavailing save in what he sought.
Like him, he thought, she would have changed,
perhaps grown more robust, hands hard, a face
with lines that spoke of sun and wind, but still
his O Koyo, still with the promise seen,
twenty years now and beauty burgeoning,
a woman lovely to be lovelier,
grown as with time she must in breast and hip,
the interest come of experience
not there when only the glad present lived
in her young eyes. How would their meeting be?
Once more they would be standing on that bridge
so fateful to them, as to O Kuma,
loving would meet and fall in love again.
Yet often too he thought of O Kuma.
Her face once comely would be motherly
and beauty went with that, 'kind' O Koyo
had called her, 'caring' too, beauty again
was in these words. And nowadays sadness
might have set beauty on her face that was
of stillness, no more now the open play
of joys and griefs on features used to speak
the slightest change of mood or passing thought,
so O Koyo had fondly said of her.
Yes, there would be the still regretting, not
alone the loved and dead but loving waste,
so much unused, save for his O Koyo.
The father he imagined in unease and lost,
stranger in a strange land, far from his folk,
listless at home when day's work let him go
and then too much the prisoner of dreams.
One day in a small valleyed village he
received one more unpromising reply,
at best it might suggest a way to go,
he was now aimless, save for his set will.

Some years ago had come there an old man
with some air of authority, and in
sad circumstance - the common lot of age,
he did not ask what circumstance - and soon
had proved his skill in judgement as in work,
so now was Headman. With him he had brought
a woman now in her mid-twenties and
his grandchild. Travelled it would seem, he might
have news for him. And so, a day's stint done,
lamps lighted in the homely scattered huts,
a meal with his informant gladly shared,
the way was shown to him, and to his knock
a woman answered, it was O Kuma.
    Never was face but one so beautiful,
and there thought paused, but she had drawn him in,
found him a place. 'Always I hoped, one day
you had to come. Here, my lord, is your son.'
'Yes,' said the old man entering, 'your son,
and he has been a long time waiting you.
See you live up to all that he expects.
Such tales are told of you, you have been here
and real as was the teller of the tales'.
Bewildered, Takoji knelt to the boy
and the small arms grew round him suddenly.
There were tears in his eyes not there before,
and O Kuma's were bright with them, and he
remembered, as in many a sad place,
that day of loving days the last and best
when O Koyo had voiced her craving for
his child loved into her, and here it was.
The boy looked up and he was wonderful.
And then the question not a question put,
'And O Koyo?'
    The father looked away
and it was O Kuma who answered him,
'I think, my lord, you must know that she died.'
And Takoji, unable to believe
the truth he knew, his voice a breaking thing,
said to the boy, 'You know your mother dead?'
'You mean the other one? "Dead" means that she
is not around.' 'Yes, not around, that's all,'
and now he rose in anger, struck the wall,
'never around, never around again!'
His voice that had been too loud for the boy

was now a whisper to himself, 'My love,
why should it kill? She knew the chance and yet
she let me love.' 'My lord,' said O Kuma,
'you frighten him.' He saw the father gone,
not able to hear more, and saw his son
staring at him. 'Love gave you him as she
had wished, it does not help, it does not help
at all to cry', but she was crying too.
And grief to grief he reached out and embraced
her, held her head to him, and there she let
it rest, and held so she began her tale.

'It happened somewhere in the hills and there
we buried her. Her pains came on so strong,
There was no help about. I had to be
the midwife, help her thrust it forth, and with
such rending strains, bite mother's cord from it.
I think she heard its first smacked cry of life,
for she said 'Takoji', thinking you there
and that my hand was yours.' 'I understand,'
he said, remembering. 'When I had cleaned
the blood from it and then had turned to lay
it to her breast I saw to the one side
her head was laid, and soon that she was dead.
No work on her could bring the heart-beat back,
it had taken too much of strain. She had
to fight too hard to win, but win she did.

'Her father buried her under great stones,
a leaning roof of stones that covered her.
He said, "Just like her mother," nothing more.
How he survived that day I do not know.
I went on till I found this village and
a wet-nurse here. People were very kind.
Someone went up and found her father still
sitting beside the stones and brought him down.
The old man, he is brave, yes very brave,
always he rises, faces the new day
as Headman, as if others' little cares
were all he knew. He works, never looks back.'
'No,' he said, 'he looks back and has to work.
One day, not now, I will believe her dead
and that day she will be, and the hurt less.'

His son had not been listening, houses
with walls and roofs, an entire village was
now taking shape under those little hands

with bits of wood. Takoji thought, life made
its children, no, not practical, that too,
but able to live in their world of play.
'Dead' means the other not around, so not
in their play-world, dismissed. Later they would
form ties, never again know a play-world,
dismiss dear loss as simply 'not around'.
He had been such a child till that day on
the Bridge, and yet he would not have unwished
that day, no more would O Koyo, even
if they had known what was to come. Perhaps
the difference was only that they knew
and yet played on. He thought of O Kuma.
What debt of life was owed those loving hands!
He wondered, did she think on a space filled
and look to happiness? Some time she had
to know his will on that, he had to think
on it. But now the boy. And Takoji
took his son off to bed, told him wide-eyed[8]
the tale of Little Peachling, and sat there
holding his son's hand till he knew he slept.
And as he sat the knowledge came, his will
was made for him, there was nothing to think
about. He would see that the growing boy
knew out of what great beauty, courage, he
was come, some day together they would see
the stones. But now he had a mother. That
decided everything, and O Koyo,
he felt, would have approved all he would do.
Back at the fireside and with O Kuma
he said: 'I need you in the family
just as you are, his mother, and that means
my woman, in my bed to breed for him
brothers and sisters. Now the old man sees
you as a daughter, they will be to him
his own grandchildren, brighten his sad days.
And there is this to say. Take no offence.
Four years I have known man's desire, and held
it in, as you a woman's, and tonight
we know relief that often shared will be
the need of love. What do you say?' 'Yes, and
still yes,' she said. 'To know my man will come,
find me his woman waiting, that for me
is happiness long and so sorely missed.

My need, it is as yours, no more, no less,
I had to wait the father of her son
or who knows in what arms I might have lain,
so much the better someone from those days
when there was Chokichi and O Koyo.
I think held in your arms that I will cry.'
'One thing,' he smiled, 'no more of this "my lord",
plain Takoji it is.' 'Yes, but my lord.'
They told the old man, all he had to say,
'It gladdens me that Takoji sees sense.'
    There had been talk of harmless, hurtless things,
round them the murmur of a sleeping house.
O Kuma said, 'Make me forget the years
and what has been,' and she forgot; later,
'Winter is gone, seedtime is come at last,
I shall be husbanded and made to grow,
and you will know the fatherhood you missed,
the old man have more children he can spoil.'
She held him tight, 'all this from labouring
a dead man's field,' and her eyes were tear-bright.
'I think upon heaped stones,' he said, and they
suddenly held together in shared griefs.
'No more,' he said, 'enough,' and they made love
till tired she seemed to sleep.
    But he thought on
and it was then the voice of O Koyo
came high and clear, so clear he had to rise
and look into each room, but nothing seen,
the old man and the boy slept sound, and still
came the clear voice: 'What of the promise now?
Death the good gardener made sure I would
be that and nothing more, never the rose
full blown. Now I shall always be in bud
and set your heart to dream. Yes, in the son
he could not win from me and that I wanted so
you still will see me grow. Not even my
loved O Kuma takes him from me and you.
Love her, my Takoji, love is her need,
her nature,' and the voice was gone. He felt
a hand and it was O Kuma. He stood
there cold and naked, and it seemed to him
he heard her last two words, 'Adzuma Bridge'.
O Kuma said, 'Takoji, come to bed,'
and then, 'O Koyo, was it not?', and when

he nodded held him close to her and said,
'You will not hear her more, I promise you,'
and in her arms almost he felt this true.
He said, 'I think that we will learn to love,'
and 'love' was the right word, his O Koyo
had used it as she went.
    Later she slept,
he lay and dreamt what children she would bear,
and as he dreamt O Koyo, O Kuma,
merged and were one, and big with promise bore
the sons and daughters of still waiting time,
differenced in their traits and gifts, of course,
undifferenced in that best trait and gift
which is the love of kind.

Notes:

1 The local governor's castle in old Honjo, where most of the characters in this tale reside.

2 A.B. Mitford Lord Redesdale, **Tales of Old Japan** 1871 says of this caste, 'Their presence pollutes the house of the poorest and humblest', injured they had help only from their own kind. Buddhist bias seems to have reserved these trades to them, yet the killing trade of the soldier was honoured. The outcasts had a supreme chief at Asakusa. Mitford's tale has the same names but is quite different.

3 Japanese women would hide their figure but these were singing-girls. The instrument would be the koto.

4 A few miles from Honjo.

5 'ronin' - one of a class of wellborn, often disreputable, adventurers.

6 For such an incident see note to Mitford's **Tales**, p.177.

7 The method is used on Christian missionaries in Endo's novel **Silence**.

8 A Japanese fairytale of a marvellously born boy who slays an ogre.

THE BOY

He thought himself a man. In a surround[1]
of violence were lived his sixteen years.
His close friend hated, he accepted it,
yet the friend knew in him awareness near
to strange, so keen it was. He heard it in
the sounding wave along the beaten shore,
thought of it in the strong birth-throes he knew
had killed his mother, she who set him to
such fond imagining. It came into
tempers that flared at school, in elders' talk,
the sudden quarrels of the marketplace
that could have deadly issue, and he thought
of the blood-debt and payment still pursued.
Was it this violence that drew him so
to women, features of a gentler world
you saw in them, and unavailing, they
were where you dreamt, near ineffectual
as the but rare-seen law.
    So you must learn
from early years the art of self-defence,
at best a gesture in the face of life
but one he made so well. A prodigy
his tutor an old ronin had pronounced,
the right aggression and the right restraint,
with shift of tactics at surprising speed,
and in his fifteenth year had given him
a sword of noble lineage to fire his zeal
to further practice. This he bore with pride
and saw himself with heroes of old song.
In his own village no one dared cross swords.
Quite tall, slim-waisted, broad of shoulder, fine
of face, he won the interest of girls
and from his thirteenth year a something more,[2]
but women somewhat older welcomed him
and in their arms he knew a happiness
that meant much more, why he could not have said.
But no stroke of romance they won from him
like that he gave to his fine-tempered blade.
The sword it was set him on his career,
but not in the so looked for way, under
a noble banner, say the Emperor's,
most favoured of his dreams. Where was it drawn

for him so fatefully? At a dogfight.
    Shirai walked the shore with his close friend
and their two dogs. The friend was not himself,
something the father whom he loved had said
cut deep, the son excelled in nothing, could
win nothing, life would always see him lose.
'He could be right!' And then the challenge came,
'A dogfight! See if mine can win.' No sense
to it, agreed a cruel sport, and now
the angry tears demanded, had their way,
the dogs were set each at the other's throat.
Hot with blood-lust that sickened as it claimed
senses and soul, sometime the masters too
were like their fighting beasts. A shouted word
to his own dog seeming about to lose
and the friend's sword was out, Shirai's life
stood on defence. The sober swordsman lived,
the friend lay dead, the first man he had killed,
and not by his intent. With something like
a last cry of despair, a loser proved,
swordless the friend ran straight upon his death
and fell from it. Shirai stared, knelt, fled,
along the way he saw the scene again
and vomited, sat down and thought. Yedo
and something military there had been
his talked of aim. The highway had to be
the path of their pursuit, and so he sought
the byways, turning ever to the hills.
    Soon he was tired and hungry, near to night
came on a house that claimed to be an inn,
odd to find such a place in that lone land
and odder still customers at that hour,
but ten men sat about and talked and drank.
After a glance they paid no heed to him.
He called and a man came, for a few coins
fetched food and drink, soon led him to the room
and bed desired. Downstairs that single glance
had taken in his sword and clothes but most
his sword, so that stayed by his side and he
lay dressed. And yet he dreamt: the dogs had left
their fighting, one whined in its puzzlement
about its master lying still, as he
himself was puzzled. He awoke and knew
for certain what had killed his friend, not his

good sword, the father's cutting words, and yet
something of guilt remained, as his friend ran
on his astonished sword it had not moved.
He would have slept again but for the sound
of a latch lifted, someone entering.
    A girl, finger to lips, was at his bed
and whispering, 'They are all robbers here
and they will come to kill, take all they can.'
A moment he considered her, pretty,
fourteen or fifteen, then leapt from his bed
and held his sword in readiness: 'Later
will be a time to tell your story, but
for now when you hear fighting leave this place
and wait for me. Now go.' He was alone,
on guard near half an hour before they came.
The first man he cut down, soon found they had
no swordsmanship like his and still would not
believe a boy could master them, and when
the last three turned to flee it was too late,
he was upon them, one thrust to each back
and ten lay dead. Trembling he stood, like them
could not believe what he had done. Of course,
he thought, it was his sword, its history
he did not know, what scenes it knew, but he
and it were one. Strengthless he reached his bed
and felt tears come. Did heroes weep like this
for the first deaths they caused? For now he knew
his friend's was not his doing but self-sought.
    He did not move when a step came, a face
looked in appalled, his host made curious
by the strange quiet fallen. 'Come,' he said,
and when the man stood there, wide-eyed with fear,
'You did not warn me.' 'No, I was afraid,
they came and took my inn, the countryfolk
stopped coming, it will be an inn again.'
'Not yet,' the boy replied, 'ready a room
with a good bed for two. I will be back.
These bodies, bury them.' And he was gone.
She came frighted and shivering, glad and
surprised as he how things turned out, yet sad
withal. He led her to their room and bed.
'Keep watch,' he said, no sooner said asleep.
    With morning she came in his arms, he asked,
'What age are you?' 'Fourteen,' she said, 'the men

liked me so young. They took me every day
into enjoyment I had never known but once.
All dead my lovers, every one. They could
enjoy me, but I could not have you killed.
You know, my body has a hundred ways
to love, they showed me all, these poor dead men,'
and she laid hands on him that he removed.
'Where is your family?' 'In Mikawa,
my father a rich merchant whose wealth grew
on dowry from a source unsaid, but gifts
and questions asked of traders when they came
helped me to guess, and at eleven years,
near mother's age when he had used her first,
I knew my own true father. In his bed
we made such happy love, his "little whore"
he called me, and from that time on what I
would be was clear. I would do things for him
he said my mother would not do. Pregnant
by him at twelve poor silly mother looked
for a romance that was not his to give,
and yet her foolishness was flattering
so he disposed of her to an old man,
at least his date for loving past. She bore
me bitterly. No man for fourteen years!
I told her about father loving me.
"Daughter and father!", she went on and on.
Why not? He was a man. Strangely she blamed
herself for all those happy afternoons.
My poor Asan, her so romantic dreams,
all those sad years at an old man's still side,
unused, and yet the old man cared for me
if not for her, his own "dear innocent".'

'And then these men came, father gone from home,
and raped us. I was terrified, of course,
but after the first three enjoyed the rest.
Mother was different, just hated it,
felt dirtied and abused, she could not share
with them the need that drove them. They could see
I did. Now they are dead, my lovers, dead!'
He thought how strange his yesterday, this talk
was stranger still. She was not simple, she
was from another world. One thing he knew,
he wanted rid of her, today they would
be on their way to Mikawa, and there

goodbye. Komurasaki was her name.
Yes, more than his dead friend or last night's work
of death this girl's strange talk depressed him, he
had made quite clear his want of interest,
to her unnatural he must have seemed
unreal, the ordinary needs unknown.
Was it the chill of all these human deaths
he meted out that kept desire so cold?
Their host was glad to see the pair go off,
gave them directions, food, a flask of wine.
As they went on he said, 'A purple mark
a little like a star, more like a flower,
is on your brow, quite beautiful, from birth?'
'One of my lovers struck me, the mark stayed
and he was sorry after, a nice man.
He wanted something I refused to give,
my foolish sentiment at first said "No",
it was the way my own dear father loved
and mother had refused him.' After that
he asked no more.
    Yet as the memory
returned of what he owed her, and he felt
the force of a peculiar innocence
that underlay her most repellent talk,
the undiscriminating kindness shown,
he found against his will a liking grow.
She could surprise him: 'Thieves and murderers
are not all bad, they have their feelings, their
profession is not chosen, things come out
against them. Sometimes loving fancies come.
One said to me, "We are hiyoku, you
and I". I asked him what he meant. "Once there
were birds that flew and flew not touching earth,
one lived within the other", and just then
he loved, we were indeed hiyoku, earth
had passed away. I kissed him for that tale.
He was so full of fancies when we loved
and if there were a poet in him death
has silenced him.' A moment there he felt
partaker in the guilt of that fell night.
They came at last, he with no small relief,
to Mikawa and to her father's house.
    The parents showed their joy, the father in
so many words, Asan the mother in

a long embrace, yet, did he fancy it,
with question in her look, remembering
perhaps how her strange daughter went, not too
unhappily, with her rough lovers. It
was certainly the mother there who held,
and felt, his gaze, the woman meant for him.
She had that beauty special to his fond
imagining of how his mother looked,
beauty that unawares had come to be
his image for desire. Gazing at her
he grew aware questions were being asked,
they wanted to hear all, he to forget.
Firmly he said, 'Forgive me, I am tired,
Komurasaki tells a better tale.'
Asan it was who showed him to his room.
In it he held her and, eyes closed, she took
kisses and stroke, wanting and yet removed,
as if she thought, this is not meant for me.
    That night little he slept, his mind on her.
She was in all respects the mother-love
he craved and dreams had shaped: older, and that
was as should be, with all that went with it;
now she was sad, for those full lips could kiss
and if she had the right man wear a smile
that past expression would be beautiful
above a lifted breast and lips - full fleshed;
and everywhere bodied to his desire,
on her a mother's plenty swaying wide,
the large outsloping belly, spread of hips,
thighs that a lover would find deeply soft
as greatly broad and have to stroke and search.
So much the woman she must have her man,
such riches and unused, how desolate!
And when she came, knelt with his morning tea,
he bade her set it down, pulled her in bed,
stroked till she broke away, ran from the room.
He had seen tears. What life was hers to lead
he glimpsed at meals, Komurasaki spoke,
a child indulged, the mother not at all.
Silence from her was the expected thing.
Next morning when she came again, and when
he said, 'Asan, I love you,' her reply
came sad, 'No one could love me,' and she went.
    Yet with the afternoon the garden saw

them walk its lanes, on a tree-shaded seat
fiercely embrace, then happy find their rest,
her head laid on his shoulder, one bared breast
in his slow-stroking hand, enough to say
'I am all yours', his kiss on it like prayer.
For some time no words came to them, they were
not wanted, they had found each other and
they were at peace, such peace as lovers know.
Kimono free she opened to his search,
soothing, exciting, after so long years
made to feel woman and a woman loved.
'My son,' was all she said, and that was right,
'Mother,' he answered, and that too was right,
mother and son in love. Happiness had
its sound in the susurrus of small leaves,
its colours in the golden lawns outspread
and the blue skies, what little time they took
from love to look on them, and the great sun
was no small part of it, if less for him
than was the sheen upon her black-bright hair.
It had to end. Upon the longest kiss
he said, 'Somehow this perfect moment makes
you always mine, my woman, even when
I go out of your life.' 'You do not go
out of my life,' she said, 'always I will
be here and feeling your fond stroke.' They rose,
she tidied her kimono and they walked
back to the house. Just once she had to stop,
hide her face on his breast, and they went on.

Late afternoon, dusk a near presence felt,
Shirai made his farewells. Longer there
only dishonour could have come, he had
stolen no fond affection for her felt.
Asan bowed formally and looked away,
Komurasaki said, 'I hate goodbyes
and this may not be one,' the father then,
'A word with you,' and the two women went.
The old man said: 'I would have made you heir
to all I have, this morning now I know
that I have nothing, for the robbers found
my cache of wealth, money and jewels, all.
The womenfolk, they do not know, but they
will be so poor, so very poor. This house
my creditors will want. One thing alone

they will not want, a doorless cottage bare
of everything just outside Meguro.
I am a fool not to have hidden well
what meant so much. Your dead men were in need,
so somewhere on their way they hid, spent, all
and I could not begin to look for it.'
'The few coins that I have will not help here.
In Yedo if luck strikes I will be back.
Be sure I care enough to come and see
how the two women fare, do what I can.'
'Spoken as I expected. My life span
will not be long I know, I am too old
to start again.' 'Good wishes never are
good money but are all that I can give.'
The men embraced, there was no more to say.
Shirai looking back could see Asan
stand at the door to see him go and sighed,
he had his sword, just then it did not help.
In days to come Komurasaki could
fend for herself, Asan would be quite lost.
He must find service, pay, leave to return.

The way to Yedo seemed so long. It was
with some outlying dwellings just in sight,
near dark and on an empty road, he found
himself beset by highwaymen and these
well armed. Against six swords his arm soon tired.
At times he would pierce this, now that, two fell,
but still they came. He heard a carriage stop,
knew that a man got out and took his part,
though only with a dirk yet usefully
since turning one attacker from himself,
a brave diversion. Once more his sword flew,
there was a cry. Absent till then the moon
came out, shone clear, three men were suddenly
in flight. 'Why should the moon so frighten them?'
Shirai asked. 'You fought,' the stranger said,
'with deadly skill, but they had seen my face.
I am that Chobei who with others helps[3]
Yedo's oppressed and so not liked by all.
And you?' 'A country ronin seeking place
in some lord's retinue, and I have dreamed
even of service with the Emperor.

'My belted purse knows I must find that place
and soon, or like these pitiable rogues

go break your law.' 'You pity them?' 'Three lie
this night that day will not see rise to know
how life can be, how good best hours. I learned
from a young girl whom thieves and murderers,
all dead, abducted for their daily use,
even such men know good.' 'And she was right,
evil most often has its birth in need,
no more, and where no common want is seen
still there is need, some reason mastering,
kindness is like an instinct, given chance.
I know, but let me help you on your way
and you may lodge with me till that place comes.'
He laughed. 'I would not want that sword ill used,
but I must warn you, Yedo's streets have seen
so many young place-seekers tiring and
at last turning for home from ways so hard.'
　　Shirai went with him, and Yedo's streets
were no less hard and tiring than was said,
no canvassed retinue, no calling at
the gates of great men, won a place for an
unrecommended boy. Luckless, amid
such crowds never so much alone,
he found a teahouse chiefly young men used,
at least they spoke to him. Over a meal
he heard of Purple Flower and her delights,
the new attraction at The Three Sea-coasts.
'Has she a mark of the same colour on
her brow?' he asked. 'Yes,' he was answered, 'and
quite beautiful.' So he had thought himself
and made her happy. He remembered too
what she had wished to be. Where was Asan?
　　The Three Sea-coasts was an imposing place,
gold-roofed, green-walled, the pillared entrance large,
as was the fee. He had to yield his sword,
a geisha's clients could be quarrelsome.
She had one now, he had to wait an hour,
then saw her, pretty and so self-assured.
'Shirai!' came her cry, and he was in
her arms: 'Always I knew you had to hear
of Purple Flower and come to taste of her
so famed delights. Oh you were never cold,
it was that dreadful night of killing chilled
your blood.' And as she spoke those practised hands
were fast undressing him to her desire.

Well, only she could say where was Asan.
Then he forgot love and Asan and all.
She played on him as on an instrument
tuning him for herself and her delight,
until he had to seize her, madly love.
At last the two lay still, he closed his eyes,
she had only begun. 'No more,' he begged,
'you are a witch, or witch or bitch the same,
you make a man forget he is a man.'
'And you,' she countered, 'you, you have not changed.'
'Let us lie still,' he pleaded, 'most your hands,
and tell me all, how you have happened here.'
    'No happening,' she said, 'when father told
us all his wealth was gone a moment there
I was so mad with my dead friends, then saw
they needed it much more than we.' He turned
and stared, but held his peace and she went on:
'Poor father, foolishly he felt a guilt,
his money that was meant to keep us in
such comfort, and supply a dowry for
his dear Komurasaki, lost, quite lost.
He never knew me, guessed what I might want,
not as my other, my true father did,
the one I told you in his loving would
call me his 'little whore'. He died too soon
and unmourned by Asan. "I was a fool
to see romance in him," she said, and I
was shocked, such innocence, how sad! And then
she said a strange thing, "In him was no child
to love or to want love, no more in you."
But my love Kita says I am her child.'
He listened, understood, where was Asan?
And still Komurasaki talked: 'So strange,
when she was raped she felt untouchable,
only a man who knew of it yet loved
would ever do. I told her your last day
you knew, strangely this pleased, she seemed relieved.
A pity that she was too old for you.'
Still he said nothing. 'So odd how she felt,
I could be sorry for her, and most strange
she could feel even sorrier for me.
    'But I forget, you asked how I came here.
My poor adoptive father, like Asan
one of life's failures, bitterly he saw

that truth, and with a knife he killed himself,
so needlessly! I had been telling him
that in our land it was deemed no disgrace,
rather an honourable thing to do,
for a poor girl as now I was to be
to sell her body for her parents' sakes.
I could not say outright a city whore
was what I wished to be. He only wept
and said, "How dear a daughter, sacrifice
so great". Asan just sat and held his hand,
said all the wrong things that just hurt the more,
how kind to us, how happy we had been
and still could be, were we not family?
He had to know it was not true for her,
she had been patient, he affectionless.
We found him in the garden, dead and free
of the harsh life he never could have faced.
Asan had a face set in stone as she
looked down, and then it shattered, broke. Such tears
for a man never loved and who never
loved her. People, they are so very strange,
always the unexpected.'
    Her own eyes
were streaming tears. It all was as unreal
as that talk in another bed days past,
when he had listened just so long and felt
he had to get away. Her voice went on:
'I had to make Asan see sense. At last
she did. What could she have done there? Nothing.
She had some notion you, the hero, might
come back, mend all. I said Yedo was where
to find you and your help, and furthermore
I needed her, someone to run to if
I could not stand the life. That settled it,
just to be needed, that was all her want.
She came along, I sold her rings for her,
the money paid her room and keeps her still.
And how she thinks she ever could give help
if there were need is more than I can see,
and why should I want help, safe and secure,
for we are valued properties, well watched,
and here we are a home, a family.
Yes, in the vacant nights no client calls
my lover Kita comes and sleeps with me.

I am her woman, she makes love to me,
love quite undreamt of.' All this proudly said.
He kissed her, 'Tell me where your mother is.'
She told him: 'She is that weak woman who
must have her man, and now must be near crazed
for loneness and for want of comforting.
She knows we have no outdoors visiting,
we are love's nuns,' she laughed, 'our Order strict.
She must make her own life as I have done,
poor stay-at-home, and she so likes a change.
That day you left for Yedo there were tears,
you would have thought she was that sorry thing
a woman widowed of her man, and all
for a new face in her dull life. Be kind.'
'You talk too much.' 'So my dear Kita says
and stops me with a kiss.' 'As I do now.'
He rose, dressed quickly, with a smile was gone,
but not forgotten his so precious sword.
    A thought had come to him, he knew his mind,
it would be acted out quite soon with her.
To his smart knock she opened fearfully,
obi untied, kimono hanging loose,
plainly thrust on as new come from her bed,
showing too much. Past her he strode, laid down
his sword and turned, and she was in his arms.
'Shirai!' said Asan, 'Asan,' he said.
There was a silence of togetherness.
To her it was a dream from which she wished
no wakening, to him life's quest achieved.
She said, 'I hoped and hoped, and you are here.
For you I came to Yedo, only you.
Still I remembered that tree-shaded seat,
a breast held to your lips, and then your stroke,
your stroke. I opened wide to it and was
no more myself, so it went on, your stroke!
Oh I was yours just then to take, but time
and place denied. I wept.' 'That perfect hour,
I said it made you mine.' Tender he kissed.
    'You are so greatly beautiful, no part
that shows the woman but is great, nothing
seen small, no little loveliness, all great.'
'But I have no great spirit, so afraid
of life, this city. Only need can drive
me out of doors, these streets so full of men,

eyes that undress and rape and follow me.
What I need is -.' 'Your man,' he said for her.
Mutely she nodded, then in words that cried
from her, 'My man beside me felt so close
at nights, to make me his, and his feel safe,
still there at dawn for me to serve and love
and serving feel me owned and in his care,
my man!' 'Hush, he is here, that sword I laid
at the bed's head, it knows its master, as
will you, obedient and happy so.
    'But now undress, our long wait is at end
and we are for our bed.' And glad she did,
as he. 'Now hear me and think what I say.
This hour, it is no ordinary hour,
it is our bedding time, for it I speak
the ritual as in my village used.
Again, heed what I say. Your hand: So now
we move, a man, his woman, to love's end,
Shirai, his Asan, whose womb will bear
him children loved. This is our day of days,
the day we will look back on, when we knew
entire each other, were of two made one.
I as your priest and household head now make
you mine, and make me yours. Obedient
now kneel and bow to me, head to the floor
in sign of an obedience complete.
Now do the same with me to our shared bed'.
He led her glad to lie in his strong arms.
The ritual would order all her life,
give her her place in his and there secure.
She knew a peace unknown to her before.
    'My priest,' she said, more than her man that meant,
and 'Yes,' he said, 'with holy charge of you.'
And that was it, all of her life she would
be kneeling there head bowed to him, and his.
In priestly arms she would be worshipping,
was that not what love meant? Others might talk
of worship she would never understand,
she understood the worship of her man,
call, she would come and serve the need they shared,
he would come in and she would know her lord.
He would not let her barren stay, unblessed,
the vine that never came to fruit, to life.
Yet one thing hurt, accepted yet clear seen

as shc were there and watched them on their bed,
Komurasaki under him and loved.
'Shirai, mother, daughter, as before
and the one man, it seems a fate malign.'
'No, fate has changed its nature, grown more kind,
for there is love in this and there is care,
for you the love, and pity felt for her.
Mother and daughter, what is that to me.
She was the way, I used it, I am here.
Feeling is all that counts, and all my love
is set on you alone, in you alone
can ever find its peace, then only lapsed.'
And setting mouth to mouth, working her lips,
stroking soft sides until the sleep of sense
was on her, dreamlike now returning hand,
he told her what he saw and hoped for them:
'You at my side and big with child by me
and to my seeming then most beautiful;
you with your many children, once more big,
waiting to welcome me at glad day's end;
nights when you take me to your open arms
and love sings in you so you sing with it;
a country town, a little country town,
and with kind neighbours for your visiting,
and more than streets for children at their play.'
A while there to his stroke she dreamt with him
then greeted him with the surprise of tears:
'Shirai, look at me, my love, look well,
I am not young, my years are not as yours.
Yet age is the least part, a pregnant child
I came to an old bed an unwished whore
and never ceased to be, unloved, untouched,
no small affection, a mere sufferance.
Why I wept at his death I do not know,
a presence lost, the custom of a face,
or that one moment death had made him real?
You cannot think what days and nights were mine,
what gnawing ache of emptiness within,
the hours ate at my nerves, and I ate too,
grew gross with it, not pleasantly made fat[4]
as women wish, I grew the bitch you see.'
He would have stopped her there but she went on,
to him a mother goddess beautiful,
not so to her. 'The bitch I have become

I now begin to like as well as loathe,
feed it choice scraps of food at all odd hours,
lie down with it and share its rested bliss.
Shirai, I may come to be the beast.'
And hatefully hands stroked breasts, belly, thighs.
'I had to show you my unsightliness,
and most, tell how I came to this.' He pushed
her on her back, 'You are just what I see.
You showed me what one poet meant by his
fond phrase, "the love of Love and his soft hours".
Where else but there should such soft hours be spent?'
'Shirai, sweet, you will not listen, but
what tale of love has a fat heroine?
    'And what will folk say? Only think of that.
"She has known appetite, she will know lust,
so beds a boy and milks him to the last."
That I could bear, but not what will be said
of you: "What can he feel but mother-love,
it takes no count of years, seeks only that
soft and enfolding fat that can create
the fond illusion of the everlost
briefly regained?" You cannot want such talk.'
    'I lie with loveliness, it looks at me,
its beauties still to say: Your face, full moon,
in the bright quarter of my heaven shines,
others but crescent grown; and in accord
that smiling round of mouth where dream my lips
is as my earthly moon; and then your eyes,
your eyes they are for me the softest eyes
that ever looked upon a man in love,
there I am lost and never will win out,
lost as I am in that fine mist of hair
fingers let loose to fall and still to fall,
outlining and not shrouding your fair form,
mist that near falls to shapely fashioned foot
and yet shows all. Oh you are beautiful!
    'Still, it is true, I seek the everlost.
I was the baby of the family,
six elder sons to my loved mother born
could not have left her breasted, bellied, slim
as the young mothers fresh from first childbed.
She died in birthing me. My father kept,
he said, an empty house, taught me his skills
of carpentry, it kept his mind from her.

A child I dreamt of her, how she would look,
she looked at me from you at Mikawa,
belly outsloping great, the spanished breasts,
hips vast, all swaying in your walk, your smile
a mother's smile. Older than me by years,
upon that shaded seat you said "My son,"
I answered "Mother", the words came to us.
Asan, you know the saying "Fat and fair",
your fat is fair to me, and in you yes
as that first time I see my mother-love.
What else was woman ever to her man?
So are you to me, mother and my love.
'But I have waited long, too long, for you,
and still our bedding is not made complete.'
She held him as she never would let go,
he must not go, such joy he brought with him.
He was in his own house and his own room,
the room was more than room, an anteroom
to a world all delight, the pure delight
attendant on creation that one day
under her lord would be at work in her.
Incestuously sweet the names there used,
once she cried out 'My son, my son, my son!',
and 'Mother, oh my mother!' came his cry.
Then he had left, and all delight with him,
they lay upon their mat remembering,
their bedding was complete, of two made one.
'Love makes you hungry,' suddenly he said,
'up with you woman, make your man a meal,
and fetch your shift, my shirt, the night is warm.'
Back by the bed a moment there she looked
on his young nakedness, so beautiful,
and deadly too she thought, all those dead men!
The sword lay quiet now and waiting use,
not waiting, asked for it. He saw the glance,
a look of pain came in his eyes, he said,
'My tutor had known killing, hated it.
Defence was what his gift was for. Defence
I found too often meant to kill, can kill
even without intent, then grievously.'
And he would say no more. The shirt he held
forgotten, as was she, he was alone
with some scene from his past. 'Love, death, the two
great opposites,' she heard him say. Sudden

she knelt to him, placed slow and firm a kiss
upon love's sword, it gave, not ended life.
He smiled, 'I know, if yours were the one wound,
the only one and man was fashioned kind
as you are made for love! But I waste words.'
She went, a mist of hair as he had said,
about her work, knew why the shift. It let
him see the sway and play of body moved,
and as expected soon he had to come,
press himself to her hips and stroke her down
while she leaned back on him to take his kiss,
their meeting eyes smiling yet serious.
    Making that meal, sitting with him to eat,
cushions set close, fond intimacies shared
while still they ate, hearing him say, 'That fat
needs feeding, eat your fill,' and doing so,
she knew with him she could be all herself
and still be loved. A little saki glowed
in them, they lay, stroked one another, were
at peace. And tidying away she felt
a happiness of home fill that mean room,
he sitting there in full content, at ease,
his woman at her work, all as should be
and had not been those many patient years.
She did not say 'Shirai, stay the night',
it went unsaid, everything here was his,
and when she heard his 'Time for bed' she went.
That night after their loving she slept well,
his hand in hers drawn tight across her side
as if for more assurance he was there,
and if at times love still made its demand
that only made assurance doubly sure.
Safe with her man she did not startle at
each one of Yedo's many passing sounds
and fear, as she had done since first she came.
    Morning found ways to enter and the room
grew light. Shirai woke, she slept, a slap
on fair fat buttocks brought her wide awake.
'Breakfast,' he said, and heavily she rose,
reached for her last night's shift. 'Leave it,' he said.
Whatever moved him would not wait on her.
Something had happened in the night, but what?
Shirai's nightmare, that was it, he seized her, loved,
loving said 'Mother', as he would but this

time as a child might cry, child-man that fled
his frightful dream in her, fought it so hard
that pleasure moaned, head tossed, and yet she did
not fully wake, and eased he fell away.
And now she asked, 'Shirai, is all well?'
'Of course,' he answered, 'but I have a friend
to visit early.' She said nothing more
and naked, soon to sleep again she hoped,
brought him his breakfast, and that eaten he
took her as if part of his morning's meal,
fondled her absently, then ordered her,
'Bar well the door, answer no call but mine,'
and he was gone, wearing his sword she saw.

Alone she thought, only a nightmare, though
it woke such need in him. With morning gone
clean from his memory. These orders too
were only care for her. Still she obeyed,
he was so much the master. For the slap,
her nakedness, he wished, he had his wish,
just as in bed he took her as he willed
so in the day in his will was her peace.
And it was good, life to be ordered so,
possessing and possessed she had her place.
In bed she thought of him, spoke to herself:
'My boy, my boy so beautiful, and I
so thighed and hipped and bellied, I am yet
for him most beautiful of women, sole
bed for his love, rest for desiring. My
young god, he bears me to his heavens where
we soar and soar. Oh we descend, my boy
and I, but to no ordinary love.
It is his mother that lies in his arms,
it is my son whose lips are at my breast,
and these names are more tender and intense
than those that ordinary lovers use,
they are more true to how things are, to how
we feel, and yet simply he is my man.'
But now a wave of weariness was come,
as she went under his dreams went with her.

Shirai had not said why he must go,
nothing of the remembered scene that at
uncertain hours would visit him, as last
night in his utmost happiness. Warm at
Asan's great hips, in comfort lapped, near sleep,

his hand in hers, indeed his day of days,
he had envisioned life always like this,
passingly thought of those with no such life,
and with that thought on lonely, lonely sands
he stood, laid out before him a dead boy
he knew so well, his own sword dulled with blood.
The dogfight started by his friend had stopped,
one dog whined puzzled round its master stilled,
the seabirds circling cried accusingly,
rightly he felt, though he could not say why.
He had been the attacked and he had fought
only defensively, and then as if
that strict defence had maddened him his friend
had thrown his sword away, himself on death.
Shaken he had knelt down, half open eyes
staring so sightless he had closed, had felt
the awful and protested fact of death,
this outwith all belief, and fled from it
as much as from the men who had to come.
With fleeing the scene went. He moaned, Asan
not waking opened to him, he went in
and loved with force then leaving her he slept,
as for that time his grief.
With dawn he was
himself again and knew what he must do,
make sure there were no signs of that pursuit
lost by his taking to the hills but here
continued, for if signs there were Asan
and he must move. Perhaps his friend in need,
his helper in that ambush of a night,
could help again. Had there been questioners?
He told Chobei of the new state of things
and his friend smiled: 'A woman in your bed,
there will be growing needs, a child asks more
than mother's milk. Take this my boy,' threw him
a purse of gold. 'It has been often said,
"good wishes are good nothings to a need".
But more than gold your want is good advice.
Keep your hand near that sword you wield so well,
this city, outward-seeming so alive
has yet an underface of death and worse.
Passion spent on your woman, that is good,
not on some teahouse whore whose fee could turn[5]
you to a thief or murderer, your end.

Penniless and no friends with influence,
my dealings are with small folk, not the great,
here is no place for you and yours. Go home,'
    But that Shirai could not do. 'Almost
I had forgotten,' Chobei said, 'days past
a tall old man with voice like yours was here
and asked for you, said he had known you well,
spoke of your fighting skills. Your tutor, tired
of court where swords were decorative things,
went back to his own place and taught the boys.
You were his favourite, a prodigy.
I liked him but knew nothing. Yedo learns
suspicion. There was purpose in him, what
you may well know. I do not ask, the less
I know the better.' 'Yes, but trust I want.
Something was forced on me, my greatest grief.'
'I understand, your sword must be your friend,'
for him a bitter irony in that.
'Until, unwilling I must speak the truth.'
And Chobei looked at him, 'I like you lad.'
Shirai was near tears, 'You have been kind
and like a father here.' 'Off with you boy,
if I can help I will.' But two months passed
and Chobei's warning was proved on himself.
He knew the risk that the set meeting meant
and yet he went alone, unarmed, to fall
to shameful spears prepared by one who knew
his spirit. Yedo's poor might mourn, the man
responsible be known, but none dared act,
yet two nights later he and his two guards
lay dead. One sword-stroke dealt with each. A boy
had visited, no boy's work this. Asan
soon guessed, tensions she felt relieved on her,
'Mother' said on her breast spoke her son's need.
'When will its day be done, Shirai, when?'
He did not answer, quiet too the sword.
    Only days later life for them was changed,
Asan had news for him, kept it for bed,
her need was now as his and bed was best:
'Not three months gone and life loved into me,
I waited, now am sure, I bear your child.
Happy I am my master called so much
and one such call enjoyed meant fruitful seed,
so now our child that all so quiet grows.

Glad I was, gladder grown with each time called,
never so glad as now.' 'Mother, I love
you with, without, a child, but father made
tender I feel and proud. Now love must learn
a gentleness not used before, more than
Asan I hold.' 'Not yet your gentleness.
Son, love your mother, for such need she feels,
this of all nights should be her night for joy.'
He moved on her, a wave upon her sea
to beat upon the shore of her desire
until delight was torment, and almost
she could have wished delight would fail, and when
it did wished it would beat again. It beat
again, she moaned, cried out, it went. Her nails
had torn his back unfelt, her belly moved
by pounding wave on wave was still. Now she
was shore and he cast up on her, nor had
he will to move, her tired and stranded love.
And yet twice more life moved. When would he stop
or she stop wanting him? And then he left
her and she turned into his holding arms.
'Little Asan,' he said, his tenderness
felt her his woman-child, the more so now.
She thought upon his son enwombed, yes son,
for seven sons his mother bore her man,
and on the months to come. 'Shirai love,
what will we do, we have such lusts, we two,
waiting our baby's thrust to life and then
the healing of my wound? Your mother-love,
she is big-bellied now and that you like,
but bigger grown, love not so easy made?
And after the fifth month there could be harm
from love's sweet violence. Will you live chaste,
gently embrace, say goodnight with a kiss,
or on Komurasaki find relief?'
'Love you as ever I have done, and in
my arms held close know you worth waiting for.'
'I will be great with fat, larded and heaped,
in all my movements slow and cumbersome
the very image of a breeding bitch,
then most I will need love, your patient love.
And yet I know I will look back and think
the happiest of times my breeding days
when I could feel, "Life uses me as meant".'

'And I would have you that way every year,
were it not selfish and bore hard on you.
And yet we know that we will always love
and you want babies coming still with love.
I will look happy on my teeming bitch,
a bitch for love to see and dream upon,
thinking how my desire and your desire
coupled in tender night to make you such,
sorry for the sad loins that leave to love
for fear of the one child too many come.
You will be beautiful for what you bear,
only less beautiful than when you lift
once more a breast for milking and are eased,
a mother's smile above her newborn child.
With it, and only then, my call will come.'
'Shirai, always we will know desire
and love's sweet violence will have its way.
Hurt me with love, wound me with sweetest pain,
take me with strength, my need will make for you
an open way.' 'A way to where? Asan,
as often as I enter you we are
right at creation's centre and no more
ourselves. I lose myself in you. As now.'
Two loves lay happy, tired, she turned aside,
drew his hand on, not theirs, creation's child.
As if out of her sleep he heard her say,
'Your whore Komurasaki has to hear.'
It was the name set him considering,
the baby had decided, they must move.
Chobei had warned him and he had delayed,
for him and his Asan this had been home.
And his pursuers had to know so much:
the boy who had avenged good Chobei's death,
and more important at the inn of death
a host to send them on to Mikawa,
not only he would know the history
of Purple Flower the much desired, they would
expect a visit, watch The Three Sea-coasts.
All things considered sleep at last approached,
and with it placeless, vague, a scene he dreamt,
the tall old man talked with him, then alone
went on, whereto he could not see. For some
odd reason he was sad for him. He slept.
Morning and his awaking brought the strong

sense of events in movement and himself
the mover. He lay tense, too tense he thought,
not how a fencer should approach his bout.
'Mother,' he called, 'I want you.' She was dressed
and at her breakfast, but she had been trained,
rose and undressed, was used, enjoyed him too,
wondered at kisses lips and body shared,
so serious and fond, answered in kind
and held him to her breast, but this was not
need's simple call, love spoke, 'You are too kind.'
A blush of pleasure mantled her round cheeks.
They dressed and more relaxed he ate with her.
Her talk was of the baby, she had thought
it moved, 'But much too early yet for that.'
    Finished with food he cut her off: 'Listen
and carefully, Asan. When I come back
we leave at once for Meguro. Danger
is here for me, so you and baby too.'
Her baby! She was all attention now.
I will explain along the way. Pack food
and drink, three blankets, two nights we sleep rough,
easy for me to shoulder. By hill paths
we go, avoid the highway where men watch.
Our goal is that poor cottage creditors
despised and my skills will repair. My love,
if I do not come back within the hour
still make for Meguro, the Temple there,'
Frightened she stared. 'Let no one in the house.
Now move, make ready.' He embraced and went.
She could have cried, this had been home to them.
    As he expected the teahouse was watched,
a man leaning against a pillar looked
at him and idled off, one of the men
who ambushed him that night, so that was how
questions came to be asked at Chobei's house.
Odd company for the man seeking him.
Komurasaki welcomed him, she seemed
a trace more sober than last time, but much
pleased for her mother's pregnant happiness:
'Though not for me, I did not know that I
could love, be loved, till Kita made me hers.
She says I am her baby and I feel
I am.' 'Why don't you set up for yourselves,
a room for two, rooms for the customers?'

'It is a scheme Kita would like, and I
confess men do not interest as once
they did.' 'Komurasaki, I am here
only to tell you that to Meguro
we go today, and to the Temple that
I have not seen.' 'Shirai, have you done
something against the law?' 'Have people asked
about me?' 'Yes.' 'Tell them of Meguro,
but not just yet about our Yedo home.
One day Kita and you should visit us.'
He kissed goodbye. The old man had to be
at Meguro and in the Temple square.
The sword was not his only weapon, truth
could cut more deep. He hoped it was not used.
    Outside the house lounged a tall man, he was
the father of the friend who died. 'You want
to know about your son?' 'Yes, and I want
the reckoning.' 'The blood-debt?' 'Yes again.'
'Then you believe against all circumstance
the one responsible should pay that debt?'
'I do.' 'And I do not. You were a man
for whom I had respect, great as for my
own father, great as for my tutor, you
are wrong, are terribly and sadly wrong.
Your son who loved you, were he here would beg
you to unsay these words.' 'He was too kind,
it was a weakness, softness, that ran through
his life, spoiled all his aims.' 'How did he die?
I ask myself the same and, though I guess,
from the bare sands the dull half-open eyes
give back no answer, or they seem to say
asking is pointless now. He was my best
of friends.
    'That sunny and so idle day
he challenged me to match him dog for dog
in the death-fight, though for that cruelty
he felt only disgust. "I have to see",
he said, "if something that is mine can win".
That day, whatever moved him, he was not
himself, his dog would find my throat unless
I played along, not thinking as it leapt
my sword had cut it down. We were both sick
with what we watched - why did I humour him! -
and yet caught up in it. My dog did well,

much better than he hoped or ever I
expected. We were shouting mindlessly,
and then his heat and anger turned on me,
I had been hot, abruptly I was cold.
Still I can see his face estranged with wrath,
his sword out-drawn and him attacking me,
forgotten all he knew of swordmanship,
his own or mine.
    'I fought defensively,
tried to make my words reach and sober him,
to spin the blade from him, kept backing off,
but just then he was mad. It was as if
years he had waited to win that one fight
or any fight, and this his testing time.
And then the final madness, he despaired,
never would he win past my guard, never,
never win anything in this man's world
where winning mattered so much to most men,
threw down his sword and with a cry he ran
on mine, for this so unprepared, and fell
from it. And there he lay, my best of friends
quite dead, the sand slow reddening. I have
to shake myself not to be there again.
I stood and cried and cried, so uselessly.
You found him with eyes closed, I closed his eyes.
Then I came to myself, fled to the hills.
And that is all.' The tall man looked at him,
'I can believe you, every word, and yet
he was my son, you know what to expect.'
He nodded and went off.
    By winding ways
that should have lost the closest follower
Shirai found his home and there Asan
fearfully smiling, all things packed. It was
no time for explanations, but he felt
sorry for her. 'Mother,' he said, 'death waits
for me, I go to meet it, it will wait
for me at Meguro, and what that means
there only will I know, you know, but how
all this began you will learn on the way,
tired as I am of telling. All my trust
is in my enemy, that he will hear
and know the truth. Then you will have your son
killer no more or fleeer from his foe,

simply himself, your man.' She took his hand
and they went on. His pack felt strangely light.
    The paths proved clear and in two days they were
in a small overlooking wood, seen clear below
the little square, great Temple steps,
and men slow moving there. Laid that night in
a windfree hollow, cold-bright stars above,
held in his arms and doubly blanketed,
made warm sometimes in the brief fits of love,
she found at last an intermittent sleep
and waking with the dawn saw him stand still
at the wood's edge and looking to the town.
A menace in that stillness came to her,
hawks see quite clear from even greater heights,
steady themselves for the unerring strike.
Yes, the clear eyes could see the pacing man,
but nothing hawklike entered that still stance,
if there is a remorseless pity that
is what he felt. He heard her move, 'Breakfast?'
he called. His voice was cheerful, not so she.
For all her fancy of the deadly hawk
she saw herself made widow, with his child
to bear, and said as much. 'But this is no
day of the sword,' he reassured, 'almost
I wish it were.' She did not understand.
Their breakfast eaten they packed all again
and left the wood.
    They entered warily
by a small winding lane that reached the square.
'Stay here with baby, keep it company,'
he smiled. 'It is not you should cry today.
And guard the pack, we will need it again.'
And easily towards the Temple steps he went,
so easily he was quite near the four
men talking when they grew aware of him.
Two were his highwaymen, doubtless now hired
to help when sword met sword, they knew him, would
not fight without the others, villagers.
Still he walked on, hands flew to hilts. 'No need
for that,' he said. 'Tell the man I have news
for him alone and words he will not like.
The matter he may well have guessed by now,
it may be why he prays. The man he is
has heard news, words, unlikeable before

and dealt with them, but never such as these.'

'Then must he hear them?' one asked of the four.
'Yes, for he will not listen to himself and truth
and still pursues me guiltless, and with me
the mother of my child. Were I alone
he could pursue me all my days, I could
defend myself and let him not admit
the truth of things. But it is not for them
alone I speak. I speak here for his son,
not heard in life, no more in death when most
he tried to speak.' And to the one who asked:
'You are his brother and most like you know
what will be said. It must be said. You knew
me in his house, surely you can believe
I am concerned for the effect my words
will have.' 'Must we hear all this talk?' asked one.
'Yes,' said the brother, 'wait', and climbed the steps.

Soon the tall man showed in the Temple door,
descended to the square and said, 'What are
these so unpleasing news and words?' 'They are
for you alone to hear and think upon.
Your brother can have keeping of my sword
the while we talk apart.' 'You seem quite sure
you have something that I should hear.' 'Hear him,'
the brother growled and took Shirai's sword.
'You told me how he died.' 'Something I left
unsaid that, I suspect, is on your mind.'
They stepped aside. 'The one responsible,
you said, should always pay the debt in kind.
I disagree, as did your son.' 'Always
he was too kind.' 'Pity for you with that
belief held still my tongue.' 'Pity for me?'
'You were responsible. You must have asked
that question many times. Your face
tells me you have. That day, just as I said,
when your son was so strange and not himself,
mad to win something, were it in a death-
fight of his so beloved dog or with his best
of friends, and failing in them both, quite lost
to sense, threw himself upon death, what moved
him to such madness?' 'He was weak, failed in
all tests at school, in swordsmanship, in life,
that came his way, and that last day he was
indeed one of life's failures. Oh I could

believe you!'

There were tears in the man's eyes.
'And who made him so mad to win that day
he altered from himself and lost all sense
and kindness that was in the friend I knew?
The father whom he loved too much, who was
to him a god, whose every word to him
was truth. Did you not know he was most liked
of all boys in our village? You might be
respected, he was liked as never you.
And he was loved by one girl. Were not these
successes in their kind? The day he threw
his life away you had first told him he
would fail in everything. What did that mean?
That you could never love him. Sore distressed,
as I had never seen him, he died on
a cry of lost despair, you had been right.
Who was responsible for your son's death?'

Shirai walked back to the four, left him
still standing there, head bowed, face turned away.
Once a hand rose as if to help shut eyes,
keep out what the mind all too clearly saw,
and once he shook his head as if to rid
it of the thought that would not go, at last
was still. A little while so he remained,
then came towards them. 'Let the young man go,'
he said, and once more climbed the steps. 'What he
must do is best done in the Garden,' said
the brother, and his face masked all he felt,
as had the father's.

'You had guessed?' then asked
Shirai. 'I had guessed, and not alone,
your tutor said, "words kill if aimed where they
most wound", and yet, give him his due, it is
not every day a father will admit
to killing a loved son who loved too much.'
'And you did not speak out?' 'Oh you were right,
he would not hear himself. Why me? I have
that same kind weakness he found in his son,
I could not kill him with the truth, not I.
But you, defence, attack, all one, a way
you think - oh I know of the ten, six more -
a few quick words to point you had him dead,
sure as with that so famous sword. And here

it is. I only came along to tend
or bury him when the admission dawned.
He should have done by now and I must go.'
    The little square seemed to press in on him,
he must get out of here, get quite away
from people and events felt so unreal.
She was where he had left her and so glad
to see him. 'Son,' she cried, and with that word
the nightmare world of winning, losing, or
in Yedo or in the mad mind that killed
a son, and menaced them, the mind's supine
attendant that would not speak out or act
either for brother or for pitied son,
had never been. But she was here and real.
'Now we are free to live and going there.'
Then suddenly, he did not know from where
the words came, or why they should mean so much,
'Promise me, mother, you will never die.'
Her answer was no answer but the best,
'Just minutes past I felt our baby move.'
His laughter of relief rang down the lane,
and the pack shouldered, handed they went on.
    'Work to be done, neighbour.' It went like that,
the scattered village made a home for them,
the woods and fields looked on, knew the next stage,
children would run in them. He had a trade,
the carpenter's, the same his father had,
his sword laid by was a forgotten thing.
Asan said once, 'Your dreams, they all come true,'
she would give birth again, her time was near.
'Life has the best dreams, just to follow them,
drift with them, make them yours, is all,' he said,
'and when they end, well, you have had your dream.
Of all its dreams, mother, you were the best.'

Notes:

1 A briefly noticed dogfight, three names, the 'hiyoku' fancy, are all that this tale owes to Mitford's very different story of the love of the murderous boy Gompachi for the enforced whore Komurasaki.

2 It is at this age that the lady Murasaki Shikibu makes Genji's affairs begin.

3 On Chobei's association the Otokodate and his death, see Mitford.

4 Early Japanese pictures show the ideal woman as more than plump, poets compare her face to the full moon.

5 This is the substance of Mitford's tale of Gompachi's love for a girl who honourably turns whore to help poor parents.

CAPTAIN NARIHIRA

It has been said, 'Most men love to one taste' -
this writer sees no grain of truth in it,
they love where they are loved, can they say more? -
'but Captain Narihira, he made no[1]
distinctions'. Yet how different the case!
Used and pursued he was, no matter, since
the last pursuit brought such a happiness.
His own pursuits were casual, save two
that moved to verse sad as their issue was.
But first to speak of use. His mother died
in giving birth. His father would not look
on the son 'drawn from death', the crying life
that had outlived its dear loved source, and in
a circle of his honoured friends steadfast
there took his life. The wetnurse, twelve years old,
in a great house left only female was
a girl of character and much enjoyed
her privileged position, so disposed
of an unwanted child and jealously
made the young Narihira hers. Into
his own twelfth year he slept with her, and when
one night he took her she made no protest,
indeed for some time had expected it.
Her place was all the more assured. Nor was
she a mere sloven, no, as ever she
bathed the young master, dressed him, saw all needs
were met, herself now one, a tutor hired
to her own taste. Handmaiden and his voice
the servants said. Soon the whole ordering
of things was hers and the shared bed that gave
her status seemed as always it were shared.
And Narihira, he accepted all,
a lonely house was home only for her.
In looks quite plain, mainly coincidence
that his last love was a like case, of course,
the nurse and he shared only a fond use.
Or use or love, woman or first or last,
critics that seek a pattern must fail
denying both. 'Your last was not the last'
I hear them say, 'what of his geisha famed
who followed him for love, and for herself
and midwifery much needed in that house

made one of his establishment?' Yes, one,
but not the principal, for those strange **Tales
of Ise** grossly lie, last love was so
much more than passing pity for the lusts[2]
of a lone woman. Yet they will go on,
'How suspect your plain nurse and love as plain'.
Romantics, poet's loves are never plain?
Why so? First fondness had its influence,
and in plain looks what beauty can be found
of feeling that makes all appearance vain
and secondary to the love there seen!
 The Narihira that is known to fame
had to outgrow himself. Two loves for their
unhappy ends helped here; their consequence
such memorable words as well up in
men's hearts and felt their own, so they will say,
'As Narihira says' and mean one thing,
'I have been there'. And all this said, confirmed,
should we not think whatever made an end
to passion as to play, whatever built
content about him and, out of himself
yet so much more himself, gave him the thought[3]
to live his many lives, meant so much more?
My tale goes with him to that journey's end.
 And first, first love or fancy's foolish hurt.
He walked his gardens, past a tall hedge heard
and saw beauty at play, a girl in song,[4]
weaving sometimes bright flowers into her hair,
yet not so bright as it. The hair fell long
and as she bent brushed dewdrops from the lawn
and the flowers danced as on a midnight sea.
Something he felt, 'Is this then how love feels?'
He had not learned felt beauty is not love,
that is for the whole person known. He tore
his cloak's sleeve gay with passionflowers,
scribed on it his first verse, his offered love:

 Young maiden-flower, you dye
 my cloak, my heart with passion.
 Division grown so high!
 Why in no true-love fashion
 must I wait here, not be
 with you, when my torn sleeve
 speaks from your hands for me?

Not bad for a mere boy, again not good.
Over it flew. A painful silence held
the air, then gales of laughter, mindless glee.
Another player and another game.
He had been laughed at! Rushed to house and bed.
There his nurse found him, drew him to her breast.
Her baby crying! Stroked and petted him,
took him to peace. 'What would I do without
you mother?' She was glad of that fond name.
Why notice thing so slight? Was gift of self
even for fancied cause ever 'so slight'?
The boy so moved, who all too readily
could love, lay himself open to life's hurt,
lived long in him. His verse as all men note
tends to the dark, his joys still hint at griefs.
And his nurse-mother was to cry herself.
Of noble race, out of his lonely hours
that still meant home he was called to the court,
there to attend upon the Emperor,
given the title Captain for that place.
His nurse wept on the night word came, he wept
on her. Of course, she had born children, twins,
and then he used to lie and watch her strip,
as had her peasant mother, to the waist,
in tireless arms a baby at each breast,
and think: 'I fed there too, and grown still had
the nightly use of her, mother and nurse
and big with child by me! Was ever man
had woman meant as much?' But that was then.
'Mother, what will you need when I am gone?'
'Most a good father. Your head gardener,
he has long wanted me. I stayed for you.
My darlings never could become your heirs.'
The reason was not one that she could know.
'They are what troubles me, my fatherhood
was never felt.' 'I spoiled you, that is all,
kept you from feeling life as most men feel.'
'He will take someone else's children?' 'Yes,
for me, and where we go they will be his.
Provide for us, all you can do.' 'Save think
on what I lose, the breasts that gave me suck
and lips now press.' 'There will be other breasts.'
'Never the mother-nurse still there to meet
my need, who was the habit of my life.

I will have lost the home, the peace, you made
for me, lost you.' 'My baby!' and she wept.
That night his loving, it was more than fond,
something he had not known had come too late.
    He rode off to a court so much unwished,
and to his first great love. A cousin of
the Empress Dowager, she also served
the Emperor, a lady of the Bed.
This the young Narihira knew, and knew
her beautiful as women he had known
had never been. In his position he
had access to the ladies' chambers, she
it was he visited. She talked of court,
its splendour, etiquette, whom most to please,
and he learned much. Perhaps his quiet ways,
his youth, won trust, for sometimes she would talk
of her commanded service, honour felt,
with what fine voice intoned the Emperor
his sutra in the hour before her use.
And Narihira sat beside her mat,
as fit for lover's use as any Bed,
and came to know that her free heart rebelled
as did his own. Yet nothing said until
one day, her theme still honour, her hand strayed
and with a certain longing touched his cheek.
It was his signal, naked and prepared
he stood, and dreading as she did her arms
reached of their own accord and drew him down.
After, she wept, still happy to be held.
'To love is better than to serve,' he said,
and all that afternoon was only love.
    Then she knew fear, well grounded as it proved.
If they should meet he had to follow her
into her bedroom and her faint protests
reduce to glad surrender, wordless joy.
So he demanded and she learned to yield:

    Love has the use of you at last,
    has lit in you such fire
    as ever burns for me to quench,
    you hear desire
    with its sweet tongues still choir,
    and when its music come is past
    hear it again.

When all is done what have we done
but what is still to do,
of our two selves make one.

Of course, another lady of the Bed
had to report them, he too often in
her room, she found there in plain disarray
and smiling from a lover's happiness.
His lot was exile, so deemed by the court,
to village life. His mother-nurse long since
was gone, with her the twins, whereto he did
not ask and knew he should not ask. They were
in comfort, that had to suffice. Lonely
he learned the craft of falconry, shared with
the bird its freedom of the skies, pitied
its trained return to glove and hooded rest.
Her lot was different. No freedom, nor
return to him, would his love know, shut in
a high tower windowless, such punishment
insisted on for sacrilege, disgrace
to her own kin. And yet the lady felt
only a grievous guilt, her womanhood
quite tamed and lost in her. So no response
to Narihira's voice raised nightly in
its song of love, heard but beyond all heed.
Perhaps one moment the last night he came:

What does the Dark Tower tell
you of my still coming?
Nothing? And do you care?
Nothing is what we share
who were in love.

What could he do for her? Nothing himself.
He wrote petitioning the Emperor
but was not heard, and so a prisoner
the girl remained till after years released
the wreck of what she was. They say that brought
before the Dowager that lady said,
'Take her away,' she could not look on her
or hear her name. One law it seemed for man
and quite another for the woman's fault,
his the right to attempt, the duty hers
still to deny what the heart wished to yield.

And yet he had not learned, again in love
and open to its hurt as joy, and this
time with a woman all too dutiful.
    Pardoned at length, used once more by the court,
a mission to the Empress Dowager
then in the West Pavilion brought in view
a beauty that among all beauties there
moved as the moon in an else empty sky.
He had to visit her, and happiness
a while was his, days of such happiness,
the little white clouds drifting overhead
in pace with his own thoughts, all halcyon
and seeming hers as well. Then she withdrew
from sight and reach, where, why, he did not know.
A lady said that she had worn a ring,
he had seen none. Removed for him he guessed,
and had she fled her feelings to keep faith?
    What are a few days perfect as they pass
when a man loves? An ever-haunting dream
that never lived to feel the touch of time,
or spoiling or enriching who should know.
It is that dream whose final going leaves
grief for best witness to its perfectness.
Another year when all that blossoms did,
when the trim gardens were a dreamer's walk,
the same Pavilion saw him stand to gaze
on vanished happiness. Here they had stood,
looked on a scene so bright, its joy all theirs.
The brightness still was there, the joy was gone,
it was not the same scene at all. He wept,
stayed stirless there till the young risen moon,
not that remembered, moved in him his plaint:

Is not the moon the same
that rose upon our skies
with sail so full, was watched
out of our windowed night?
Is this not the same Spring
and sun that saw us rise,
look with the morning light
into such happy eyes?
And surely it is I
that from each lovely thing
heard the unuttered sigh,

the language of our loves,
beauty that could not cease?
No, all is changed, quite changed,
and these were other days,
other the two that loved.

The Captain could not know with his lament
he said goodbye to one self, cleared the way
for entry of another and, of course,
it was a woman who new-made his life.
When men will say of Narihira, 'he
made no distinctions', they most have in mind
the love I now relate, and yet therein
he made distinction great and from the heart.
True that between the loves that had possessed
him utterly and to sad end, and for
some time thereafter, women he would use
for a forgetting. Some of these would say
that in their arms they were his comforters.
His offices of court he now resigned,
the title was for life. His sayings of
these days are from a country of the mind,
a scene, life finds too bleak. One such is this,
'Always comes the impossible, to all
a time to know a loved one's death and find
the forced belief still unacceptable,
so with love's loss that is a little death.'
It may be thought he spoke of his two loves.
But I delay and his last love untold.
Out on the moors, his falcon waited for,
he felt his bridle seized, and by a boy
thirteen or so: 'Captain, folk call you kind
and to no woman cold of heart. I speak
now for my mother, widowed at my birth.
I have two elder brothers but between
us scarce more than a year. We are all housed
and bedded now. She told us of a dream,
a man showed her affection, and that was
her word. He was she said, so much like you.
And my two brothers said, "Have you no shame,
near thirty and not past lewd dreams like that?",
and went off to their girls. I looked at her,
not really old, lone, sad, just company
I felt was what she asked. She spoke of you,

a man of feeling, and so here I am.'
A shadow in the sky, was he once more
life's prey? 'Leave me to think on this,' he said.
    That night he found her cottage where the boy
had said, in a surround of trees and lone
as its sad owner. His horse safely tied
he entered, calf-skin boots made little sound
and soon he found the bedroom by its light.
She bent above a chest of clothes, her wear
only a clinging shift of silk, so warm
the night. Pleasantly fat at every point,
neck, shoulders, waist and sides, wide hips and thighs.
If when she turned breasts, belly, were as he
expected, every part would sway in walk,
men's eyes would follow, women envy her,[5]
a man might see in her love's bed prepared.
She turned, 'Captain!' 'Take off your shift,' he said.
A moment, and she drew it off. All as
he hoped. How smooth her fat to eyes, caressing hands!
Strangely he had assumed as beautiful
a face. Round, fat and smooth, but oh so plain.
He could not see expression move on it,
nor smile nor feeling there have its due force.
Affection he had known for one as plain,
and the boy's words came back, 'just company',
so much alone, and was not he alone?
He moved into the room, 'You wanted me,'
and she was in his arms and weeping there.
He felt the belly pressing and he stroked,
if life had sides like these, texture so soft!
    'Daily you passed, daily I looked for you,
and the dream took such hold, such hold on me!'
Then almost with a cry, 'So many years
without the touch of man, unnatural,
and you so much the man upon your mount,
the horseman ever riding through my dreams.
I am a woman made to serve her man
and serving feel affection like a stroke,
be happy for its presence, if just that.
That was my dream, now you will want to go.'
'I want you to pull off my boots,' he said,
and sat upon the chest. Puzzled she did.
'And help me to undress.' Not puzzled now
her face showed the expression he had missed,

and gladly they embraced. Her sleeping mat
took them on that strange journey lovers go,
its end soon reached. 'I could have waited years,'
she said, 'been lonely many nights, at last
to feel these holding arms, my Captain's arms,
take me where I have been and know myself
a woman once again, and give a man
his peace.' 'But something more you meant.' 'Master,
pleasure like to a pain is wonderful
but is still less than an affection shared
where presence of itself is everything.'
'As love,' he said, and in her violent
tried to forget, cancel all thought of love.
Only her cry out of the agony
of a still coming and unsparing joy
brought back the plain face never to know love,
and pity moved him so, held in his hands
it took his kiss. Her smile had beauty then,
'That was your kindest act,' sadly she said.
'Tell me about your man.' 'This only, we
were chosen for each other, knew what that
would mean, I would obey, keep a clean house,
feed him, be used before he slept, and bear.
I think he loved elsewhere. He died so young.
So little feeling we had shared. Later
I thought how it should all have been, was not.
Affection more than love is woman's need
and I think too is man's.' 'And it is mine?'
'I read your poems, passing good, but all
of love and passion they are sad, since these
are short-lived things. Affection lasts, it means
a home feeling makes such, a way of life
where woman finds her place serving her man,
where he knows she is his, still there for him,
a well companioned peace, no uttered word
is needed there, such understanding reigns.
So the day passes pleasant into night
where bodies meet and shared concerns find sleep.
This may seem dull to you, I dream of it.'
'You dream a day something like one I knew,
where the nurse, mother, lover, you would be
made smooth my life, and full as then I thought,
happy indeed as never happy since
in quite that cared for way. My loves, the ones

that made me poet, they were both short-lived
and both sad-ending as you say, and yet
while they endured I lived, intensely lived,
and they have left to me an after-life,
sad yes, but one I would not be without.
Poetry was then the very stuff of life,
what it was made of and there to be used,
and if a joy imagined still I find
I owe it to those days that knew such joy,
to its companion loss as much I owe.
The riches of affection may be real
but they are poor to those that love enjoys.'
He kissed her lips again, the eyes stayed shut
as if in hopelessness. He knew she wept.
Riding away freedom he felt was his
to love, to suffer, feeling to create,
and yet her dreamed-of day went with him too.
    Evening's verandah was his peaceful time,
not now, and he knew why. His gardens spread
brought him no calm, their lovely order was
still order and too much akin to that
so lately spurned. And the vast moors that spoke
for the free spirit, falcon-wise that sped
to the horizon limitless, they did
not help, their vastness too somewhere had end,
the sky-bird still came back to hooded rest.
His images of freedom faltered, failed.
And still there was the hunt's free-riding zest,
and he was not her horseman, her dreams his!
Somewhere were waiting love, and verse its voice.
A movement glimpsed along a garden path,
he rose, not far away the woman. 'No!'
he cried. Hurt if it must it had to end.
Something quite simple and felt like a whip.
He raised his voice and anger sang at her:

I once knew a plain woman
    and oh but she was plain,
I shut my eyes and kissed her,
    still with the morning plain.
She asked, could she be with me,
    call, at my will she'd be,
but life was out there waiting,
    and love expected me.

The words, they must have reached her and the whip
been felt, heavy between ranked flowers she fled,
through garden gate and out onto the moors
heedless of bush and brier, scratch and rent.
A moment moveless there he listened, sighed,
'She brings out the worst verse in me,' and fetched
his horse. They found her crying, stumbling on.
There he made kneel his mount and set her up.
Held by one arm she sobbed into his breast
the whole way home and to her sleeping mat,
still sobbing when laid gently on her back.
How had that ever shaken belly made
its way on that wild track! So desperate.
He lay with her, pulled the skirts up. Yes high
inside the left thigh a red score, and low
under the great belly worse. Passive she lay
and stared at the night's foolishness,
but the sight had inflamed him, he made love
and found himself held tight right to the end.
Dead loves, imagined ones, went out of mind,
she was here now and real, to be enjoyed.
Nor was it only that as he soon found.
They sat, held hands. 'Only a toy, a doll
you can undress.' 'Much more,' he said, and she
'I was a fool, a fool, but here alone
after last night was more than I could bear.
The horseman of my dreams you rode away.'
'Both fools, I the unpleasant one. I struck
you in the face, brier and bush, they were
my welcoming. And your son called me kind,
a man of feeling!' 'But you are,' she said,
'or you would not sit there and say these things.'
Surprised he looked at her, she was herself
again and even felt for him. Somehow
just then she was much more than plain, not in
appearance but in what she was. He heard
himself say, 'Will you be my woman?' When
she answered 'Yes' again he was surprised,
this had been what he wanted and had fled.
'His woman', words he liked, possessing, free.
'Then I will play your game, the one you call
affection, you will make a home for me.'
And this time the plain face that smiled at him,
wholly transformed was really beautiful.

'You know I do not love you.' 'That I know
but time will bring affection, I can wait.'
'Meantime that boy of yours who caused all this,
he and his bedded bride can move in here.
Get dressed, for now you come to live with me.'
    They rode, she held in front, to the great house
and there went to the nurse's room, still his.
Her sores he salved, 'Now I am yours,' she said,
and was. 'You wanted me to make a home,
I am your home.' With each day more he felt
indeed she was. He lived as with the nurse,
his she was in the bath as he was hers
at dress, then her great child. To bear his son
was her one dream. Her baby at her breast
he would not think her plain. And he knew well
her craving, and 'Affection's child,' he laughed,
'what better reason for your way of life,
but now your own plain self to my desire
is beautiful, your shape, more womanly
than any shape I see. It is my need.'
    Made mistress of the house, for such a charge
she felt her simple dress unfit, and one
day searched among the nurse's things. The search
found wear to fit the part, though it so checked
the flow of fat she was, but then he liked
pronounced the female features, this should please.
The plain face, somehow not so plain these days,
the undress, dress, silent he watched and then
exclaimed, 'My nurse! And how I wish you were
not, were the Yuko of last night whose name
soft said was tender on my lips. Never
could I have wished to see you look so like
the woman a mere boy turned to in bed,
one fond of me as I of her, but who
still babied me and held me in, possessed
me with the ever ready use of her,
and had not the court called would have denied
me freedom, life, and my vocation verse.
The spoiling she confessed to our last night
when pity made me glimpse what might have been.
No, be yourself!' At once she shed her clothes
and ran to him: 'Hold me, my master, you
will never know what your wish means to me,
for your affection for myself I want,

not for a memory. And yet I too
would do the same dear offices as she.
I am your woman,' and she knelt. He raised
her into his embrace, 'And I your man.'
More then he might have said but stopped and left.
    That evening in an arbour the two sat
close cushioned, his arm round her, her head laid
on him, breast bared to his possessive stroke.
A fiery sun was setting, flaring wide.
She said, 'A fire more gentle burns in me,
it does not set, hand does not make, use quench,
its sweet unease, still it is there, something
it asks, one name I will not give it, yet
it comes. In short, I do not understand
myself at all.' 'Why name it? That it knows
desire is all you need to know, as I
do now. More at another time we both
may ask, not now. Relief knows but one way
that poorly, briefly serves, and it we take.
Yuko I want you in the way of man,
and you want me in your own woman's way.'
Scarce seeing and not speaking they went in.
    Clothes gone they stood and close, close, close embraced,
smiling he said, 'I think of our first night
and of your haunting image, I was then
for you your horseman, you my mount, and as
in all good horsemanship we were as one,
rider and mount, that is all I will ask.'
They lay, he covered her, something there was
he wished to say, 'My Yuko' all he said.
And she, she held him, knew in moments she
would be the helpless subject of delight,
great power would use them glad to be so used,
and to what end neither of them would know,
as to what end the life that came in her.
Who could say that, except that it was good?
She prayed for it, and still in prayer opened
herself to him. He entered, and the power.
    He woke to find her offering his tea.
'You first,' he said, and found she was prepared.
Why was her face become so beautiful?
He knew, their living, loving, all was there
and still he had to play affection's game.
The daily rites performed, 'The moors,' he said,

'my sad old falcon must be wearying.'
'I do not see you writing, my dear lord.'
'No, for I need a grief, complaint to voice
and these are gone with you, nothing to voice
but happy days.' 'Then why not that, or else
the griefs, complaints of others?' She was grown
quite earnest. 'I will see, and now the hunt.'
    But it was not the same, nothing was quite
the same as it had been, even he could
forget the falcon's flight and the trained bird
speed back to find no arm outheld, no glove
for rest, so absent were his thoughts. For him
returned he knew she would be waiting, as
if there had been an interim of life
till his alighting and so long embrace,
that now she took unsmiling and eyes closed.
And still they did not call their feeling love,
why should affection not have need as great?
And yet their loving in the nights had such
a tenderness, his eyes long lost in hers
as hers in his, as if a giving then
took place. The bath they shared saw them as lost
in one another, and her ritual
of dressing him was felt as worshipping
the body dressed, yet he could not protest.
    One day she knew something was changed in him.
On the verandah he had paced, then sat
and quickly wrote. When he came in he said,
'I call this "Lines to Yuko" and love speaks':

> You are the home of my heart,
> and you the heart of my home,
> in you I live and love
> never from you to roam
>   and be apart.
>
> In you is love's fair city
> and its most holy shrine,
> say there one prayer for me
> and may your prayer be mine,
>   to walk one way.

    Tears filled her eyes, 'You honour me,' she said,
'and give affection's prayer fit utterance

though from a lover's lips.' 'Yuko, you sleep
or did not hear me, these are lines of love
to you. Let us give up this silly game
you call affection, we are fast in love
and have been many days. It is love's child
I want from you. I cannot play your game.
Or you will leave my life and break my heart,
or say "I love you".' 'Then I love you. Oh,
dear heart, I say the prayer that women say
who would conceive in love, and scarce can wait
its answering, so much I love. And yet
I fear this love, borne up so high upon
its wave of happiness we have to fall
to shallows on the shore of days. And then
it is affection will be there and warm
in us remembering. We want them both.'
'Forgive me but I had to hear from you
what I say now, "I love you". You will hear
it many times.' She did and happily.
    Home from their sunset walk happy returned,
naked beside their bed they stood embraced,
ready it seemed for love, yet he delayed:
'Had you not answered as you did today
what happens now had never been. You could
not know it, but the words said then allowed
an ancient ritual to live again.
This is the night of all nights that for us
means most, and for its ceremony set
by who knows what strange head of family.
I fail in one thing but I cannot wait.
You should have born to me a son, I hold
your offering, all three bare as when love
was made, the child conceived as it was born.
Now by the bed where you give birth, the night
sole witness to my deed for no priest comes,
I put upon your hand my mother's ring
as handed down by women gone before.
It makes you mine for life, it makes me yours.
The ring does all, means all, it makes us one.
It is never to leave your hand. And now
for all dead women that once wore it pray.'
They knelt and prayed. 'Last rite is love, seals all.'
She could have cried on him but said, 'My lord,
it is the best of feelings to be owned,

and sealed to love.' 'And so I feel,' he said,
'but now we love, your womb will bear my heir.'
Duly sleep came to him, not yet to her,
a little longer she still felt the ring
and for it felt his seed in her must live.
    Next day the oldest servant noticed and
he bowed, 'So long since master's mother died,
we have a mistress now and I am pleased.'
She smiled and gave the orders of the day,
but thought, 'the nurse passed over and myself
before the ring'. Indeed a new respect
was in the house and shown by visitors,
all for the green stone in its ancient gold.
Questions about the ceremony she
soon learned to put aside, some strangely said,
'It must feel good to know you bear a son.'
All bowed above the ring, some even kissed.
And when he heard he said, 'All as should be,
tradition says St Kamo blessed the ring
and with it all the women of our Line.'
Once when she voiced some pity for the nurse
he said, 'She never could have worn it, or
her children been my heirs. No love. Better
her so convenient gardener - I know
your thoughts on that - provided for and more.'
She said, 'Forget her, every woman is
a nurse and mother to her man, and see,
my baby at the breast', for she had pressed
his lips there and a moment they took hold.
Happy with her he felt his house made home,
she came into a room, peace came with her.
    So the days passed he found most pleasantly,
her presence grew on him and could be missed
more than he would have thought. From household chores
that took her from him and were grudged she learned
to come at call, and her need was as his
so that she sought him out, he understood.
More often they would sit, simply content
to let the quiet time talk round their loves.
But day's end saw them happiest, for then
the garden's peace was theirs. One evening
he said, 'Love poets are conventional,
a lip, an eye, a brow, a rose-bud breast,
never a belly in their beauties' list,

yet yours, it has the heavy gentle sway
of summer seas, all of life's pregnancy,
its promise, moves with it, and seeing that
so gentle sway, as the first time we loved,
my hands go out to stroke. She listened, smiled,
but past him she looked on the child-faced moon,
St Kamo had been kind, surely a son.
She touched the ring, said the thanksgiving prayer.
Day's end, her womb so blest, could she ask more?
But just a little she would wait, make sure.
An argument on plum and cherry, which
the lovelier, no argument, then bed.
    Who would have thought that happiness like theirs
was cause for a complaint, but so it was.
One day he said: 'I try to write, I look
over old verse correcting this and that.
Here is a little and unhappy thing
that in the West Pavilion came to me.
A lady there would walk with me the lawns,
the blossom-haunted lanes. She hid her ring
then had a change of heart and left some hurt,
also some lines, such easy-coming verse,
or easy seeming. Where now is it gone?'

I have had many thoughts of you
    and they all end in one,
that I have been the walks with you
    green and beneath the sun.

This is a simple thing to say,
    but I loved simply too,
it does not help to have many thoughts
    when they are all of you.

'I want a subject, or I have it, you.
If you it is near perfect happiness.
Perfect? But the unquiet spirit says,
"Here is no place for me, why say that you
are happy? Why not simply be?" And so
the theme is lost. And true, aimless I drift
as drifts a summer cloud, all placidly,
nothing in me that seeks relief in words
that is not better spent, enjoyed in you,
indeed at happiest speech falls away.

No griefs, no raptures, ours is a still state,
no feeling asking the control of verse
ever came out of that. The one I wrote
said all I had to say, that one brief need
put life into my pen. And so, my love,
while this want works in me I am no use
to you or to myself and home is not
where I should be; "never from you to roam"
was meant, it proves just one more poet's lie.
  'This you will understand, poems they are
like children crying to be born, few come
with ease, many stillborn, even the best
need help.' Something she would have said and did
not say, and he went on, 'They are conceived
and born of an unquiet thought, where an
excitement of the heart is found, perhaps
unhappiness, but there I have to be.
Words of your own keep sounding in my mind,
'the griefs, complaints of others'. She looked down,
it might have been the ring that spoke at last,
'I am your woman, always I am here.'
  He rode off through the morning mists for court
and knew she watched him go and how she felt.
Friends welcomed him, asked what he wrote of late.
'Nothing,' he said, 'that is why I am here.'
'Kyoto has its lovely ladies, each
well worth a verse.' 'Mere passing things, affairs.
I want my heart engaged where people are,
homes where folk care and suffer, as rejoice.
I want to know the questions these men ask
of life, their women most.' And when they stared,
'Patience, my friends, I have not changed that much,
the subject still is love, but what to say
and how now puzzles me.' 'That I can not
believe of Narihira,' one replied,
'but what you seek you will not find at court,
the town and teahouse talk is more the thing.
Just go and listen when men most are free,
over the saki. Make a geisha talk.'
They laughed, 'When she is not too busy she
will wisely say, "Well, there are men and men".'
'Try The Green Shutters,' said another. 'But
such talk of poetry, it is time to dine.'
  Oh yes they knew, were of the court, and it

was not for him, strangers were made of friends
with its too guarded talk, and he could feel
tomorrow if he rode away no one
would miss him. Selves were never bared, just like
their decorative swords not to be drawn,
not used. Or was it he was changed and saw
all different? The lady wept for in
the West Pavilion he recalled, wondered
for what he wept, for all loves fugitive?
Not her. Indeed he had begun to doubt
if in these early days he ever loved,
wrote verse he truly felt. The Tower he saw
in all its boding stillness, much less clear
the prisoner pursued and made to share
his fatal lusts. Now his companioned nights
found feeling fled from him, two bodies met,
the lovely ladies that he brought to bed
the morning sun disparaged both in looks
and what the night had meant, all meaningless.
And Yuko, waiting, his stay profitless!

And still months in Kyoto he stayed on,
went where men freely talked to him, so close
a listener: of the once loving girl
discarded for unworthy reasons, with
them hauntingly; the love that never spoke
out, could not now; the partnership
of age, presence sore missed, life's empty house;
the bond enforced, where memory still lived
its parted love, its solace geisha arms;
the other woman; the son lost. Why? Why?
He came to know that tunes the happiest
had yet an under-burden heard as sad
when the heart listened, not the mind alone,
and best of all tunes were the plainly sad.
Such simple knowledge given little heed
and always there, so that some part of it
entered those dark self-portraits done in verse.
Such 'self-expression' for so small a self!
Each of us lived with, in, so many selves.

At last the truth, and now? A geisha's tale
decided all, the form it was to take.
She lay beside him, lived again her fate:
'I was a girl when one more crying need
sold me to The Green Shutters. Still I see

my mother's thin-worn breast, her child at suck,
my father's beaten look - he could not keep
himself from her or she from him - my love,
face set for our goodbye and his back turned.
How we felt then a poet has to know.
Another girl lies at his side this night,
has born the baby that should have been mine.
I wait for the new day's next customer.
Imagine us, two figures in a mist
and drifting from each other helplessly,
and looking back to ask, how can this be?
'That is the poem of my life, a tale
for you to tell, set to as sad a tune,
not beautiful, sordid some well may say,
and yet there is a pity hovering
above all human weakness and its need
that is entirely beautiful, that you
may reach and bring to what you write.' 'Koma,
you are more poet than myself. Your tale,
it will be written, you will hear it sung.
I owe you a night's loving, you and not
the geisha.' That night was not meaningless,
the morning sun did not disparage her.
And so the heart's excitement he had sought
he found in other lives, and to old tunes
set living lines, by the unaided voice
or by the koto's strings accompanied,
sung or in city street or country lane,
in laboured field or where men cast the net,
even at court, a people's poet now,[6]
though when so called he would insist 'My own,
for more of me and that the best is there
than in those bits and pieces of one self.
A poet's subject is this diverse life, and that
means many lives.' Time proves him right, his tales
just like his 'Geisha's Song' go everywhere.
Bought from her owner, no more geisha now,
some minutes quite forlorn she watched him go.
'You are a fool' the owner said and she
agreed, her way was to a home and life
despised, still she went on. Father now used
sister as mother, both with child. Not long
she stayed, one day walked out, walked till she found
the Captain's place. But how she served him and

its mistress glad of female company,
as concubine in his establishment[7]
bore him a child, Yuko, to whom the ring
kept faith, as much its mother as was she,
does not concern us here. Her place is song.
I turn to the day after her tale told.

He knew relief, all he had come for won,
so much learned he could use and keep his word,
no further need to roam. So long away
but all said she'd forgive. He knew himself,
his heart would never stray, it beat for her.
And so, all thoughts, all feelings, gone before,
the new day breaking bright, on every wind
a promise seeming borne, he rode for home.
It was not summer, yet from every bough
plum blossom spoke its lovely language and
the cherry too, and underneath the boughs
he and his woman walked. So full of love
under a tree he had to stop and kiss,
and sweet fulfilment then it seemed
just to do that, no more, as she had felt,
eyes closed in full self-gift. Their steps retraced,
'Cherry or plum, which is the lovelier?',
she asked. Beauty was worth an argument,
but no, oh no, not now, there would be none
about love's beauty when they met, embraced.

At last his house in view. You would have said
she had expected him. No sooner heard
the hoofbeats than from the verandah she
was bowing welcome in his favoured blue,
noticed, but one thing seen he saw alone,
she was with child. 'Master, you must be tired
after your ride, I go to make your tea.'
'Stay there,' he ordered, mounted the broad steps
and with her laid his hand where the child grew,
'How many months to go?' 'Four weary months.'
'Lift up your head.' The tears coursed down her face.
'I cannot help but cry, they are the tears
of happiness, I carry my lord's child,
he is come home.' 'You did not tell me when
I rode, left you alone.' 'I could not keep
you from your quest, baby and I could wait,
you would be back.' A moment there they were
one little world, he held her as if so

his arms held everything life had to give.
And then he was himself, her time drew on,
'Must I wait out these four long weary months?'
She laughed and took his hand and they went in.
Indoors as silent an embrace. As he
had said, at happiest speech falls away.

Notes:

1 In the **Tales of Ise** this was said of Narihira, courtly gallant and poet 825-80. But my tale is fantasy: the parents, nurse, 'last love', geisha, role as people's poet. His verses merely provide ideas for my own poetry, the last three poems wholly mine. See note 2.

2 It was this odd incident that made Narihira interesting and suggested my very different story.

3 This development occurs much later.

4 In Keene's excellent anthology there are two girls. Fancied love for both defeats imagination. Only the main part of the first verse sentence is in Keene.

5 This early Japanese ideal of woman has been noted in 'The Boy'.

6 The concept of a people's poetry is no more Japanese than English, it is Scottish and eighteenth-century, buds in Robert Fergusson, flowers in Robert Burns, is related to Scots ballad and tradition.

7 There was a principal woman, here Yuko, and concubines. See my tale 'The Go-Between'.

SCOTTISH AND OTHER TALES

The Land of Balladry

THE LAND OF BALLADRY

Cut are the trees, the bushes gone,[1]
with them the lovers too,
the lad and lass that handed walked
from friends' and strangers' view.

And still the name of Lovers Lane[2]
remembers lass and lad,
ages of lovers that went there
and there were passing glad.

So long time since in Lovers Lane,
so many seasons past,
we walked. One year's bright season came,
springtime, it was your last.

Times there are I could wish I were
where flowers are laid, not grown,
since what a presence missed can mean
only these days have known,

or under brave embattled bush,[3]
each golden point arrayed
against the heavens someone said,
'There a good end was made'.

And where indeed for love like ours
could place and time be found,
your side forever by my side,
but under the cold ground?

★ ★ ★ ★ ★

We should have lived in Balladry,
you worn your grass-green skirt,[4]
by you I should have slept so sound[5]
nor felt my deadly hurt,

when in and came your seven brothers
with torches burning bright.
Little they needed torches, they
who came from death's dark night!

I should have started in your arms

with the seventh brother's stroke,
still my half-open eyes not seen
by you till the day broke.

I should have come from out the grave
clay-cold, clay-cold for bliss,
you offered to my pale pale lips
your red red lips to kiss.

I should have said, 'One kiss, my love,
will twine you of your breath,'
and you replied, 'Better that kiss
than this lone living death.'

And so we might have met the fate
one night of loving gave
and when the cock crew hand in hand
walked to our common grave.

* * * * *

Such are those tales of Balladry
that end beyond the sun,
sad for a happiness felt real,
lost as by everyone.

Again, what shall we say of this?[6]
Your seven brothers come,
in hot pursuit behind we hear
the feet of horses drum.

And I dismount beside the stream
and slay them one by one,
and take my wound. You ask of me,
my last fight fought and done,

'Why does the stream run red, so red?'
I say, 'No need to fear.
'Tis but he shadow my scarlet cloak
casts on the water clear.'

And at my mother's door I fall,
where I was born, to die
and leave my womenfolk to ask
reason of a blind sky.

And soon of grief you die for me,
  but yet our love endures,
out of my side the red rose springs,
  rises and twines with yours.

I ask, what shall we say of this?
  Roses are pretty wit,
but love knows no such roses grow
  from the earth thrown on it.

* * * * *

And there is a yet sadder way[7]
  love its departure takes,
nothing so open, comes a day
  the widowed heart awakes.

For love once felt eternal goes
  though none may see it go,
such little things a warning give,
  little and hardly show.

Or much too pliant it may bend
  as to the wind the reed,
still loving listen when it should
  never have given heed.

So might in Balladry a voice
  carry its pain too clear,
a lover with his mistress speaks,
  voices of grief and fear.

'Why do you look so sad, so sad?
  Sweetheart, come tell to me.'
'Oh I have torn my good green gown
  that was so fair to see.'

'Why does your heart beat fast, so fast,
  sweetheart, my sweetheart, why?'
'Oh I have seen the falcon swoop
  killing from a clear sky.'

'Why do you sigh so sore, my love,
  why do you turn away?'
'It is borne in on me all joy
  must have its ending day.'

'And why should such sad thoughts be yours
 and turn you from my side?'
'Do you not think that the great sun
 is lonely so enskied,

the moon too with the stars that crowd,
 the night so bright, so bright?'
'And what put that thought in your head?
 It was not a lone light.'

'Oh I have seen the winter's deer[8]
 eat of the wild wild rose
and thought that beauty makes no food,
 elsewhere heart's hunger goes.'

'I do not understand you, dear.
 Still you turn from my side.'
'Ask me no more, my father dear
 came by and bade me ride,

and no more have to do with you,
 lie, talk with you, nor write,
and so said my good brother too,
 my mother waits this night.'

'And what said you, my own true love?
 Sweetheart, my sweetheart, tell.'
'That I would do as they had said,
 though it for me were hell,

never from you the one kind kiss,
 never on loving earth.
Thank God love was the only child
 between us brought to birth!'

He looked into her sad-set face.
 So loud the waterfall.
She shut her eyes on tears and knew
 the last name he would call.

Bowed is the reed before the wind
 that all too pliant was,
nor will it spring, grow tall again,
 too easy swayed to loss.

One morning she was on the hill
    and at the waterfall,
and her feet did not stop, went on
    and no one heard her call.

Today the rock from which they leapt
    is known as Lovers Leap.
Father and mother, brother too,
    let them still soundly sleep.

★ ★ ★ ★ ★

And yet that ever changeful land
    might have known gladdest times
far from the noyous talk of towns
    or jar of churchbell chimes.

In Balladry we might have fled
    to greenwood bed and bower[9]
and there so happy, happy been
    with love to tell the hour.

Oh 'twould have been a merry life
    to hear the skylark sing
and as its notes fell through the air
    know love would not take wing.

You would have born such bonny babes,
    so bonny laid to breast,
I marvelled at the little lips
    so firm, so fierce they pressed.

Your smile above them it had been
    more beautiful to me
than blossom that still grows in grace
    on plum or cherry tree.

For me the green you would have worn,[10]
    sometime the Elf Queen seen
and wondered at the long long look
    she cast, what it could mean.

But I'd have known and knowing you
    nor mist, nor sleep, she spelled[11]

would have had power so that I lay
    in her enchantments held,

no lips moved without will of mine
    to kiss her lips so free.
That way I must have gone with her
    her silent world to see.[12]

Seven years from you would have been hell,
    one of the living dead.
No, I could never have left you,
    our bonny babes, your bed.

Let others at the midnight hour[13]
    go hear the bridles ring
and see the Fairy Court ride by,
    the night for us will sing,

sing in our good green bower where I
    hold you in heart so high,
you, only you for dearest love
    until the day I die.

Cast your green mantle over me[14]
    for I would be your man,
as I have been since first we met
    and first this love began.

★ ★ ★ ★ ★

In the greenwood men talk with trees,
    tell what love they have found,
the word upon one lover's lips
    it was no empty sound,

and if it was no wedded love,
    free and unhallowed was,
yet it was of the good greenwood
    and followed nature's laws.

He lay beneath the hawthorn tree[15]
    that knows and answers all,
he asked what happiness should him
    and his true love befall.

'Where on our death-day shall we be?'
    'Why, in another world.'
'And where will that be, sweet green tree?'
    'With fallen angels hurled.'

'And what have we done to deserve
    hell and its fires and pains?'
'Why, like a desert she has flowered
    under love's springtime rains,

and glad she is, yes glad she is,
    glad from her wanton heart
that you so well have laboured her
    and made the new life start.'

'And why should things as innocent
    as children are be crimes?'
'For the live womb high heaven ordains
    holy, unholy times.

You were not wed in holy church,
    heard choir like angels sing
the glory that is wedded love,
    saw hands that blessed the ring.'

'We were not wed in holy church,
    heard choir before us sing,
but there was glory in the love
    covered us with its wing.

And when death comes the ring I gave
    under the greenwood tree
will shine as bright as any ring
    and speak as faithfully.

Oh were the pains of hell so great
    time were an endless wrack,
still from the brink of heaven glad
    to her I would come back,

come as I know that she would come
    were I to cease from breath
to give the only kiss of life
    would win me back from death.'

'Fools you are,' said the hawthorn tree,
'no greater fools I've known,
yet I could envy you the love
makes you feel less alone.'

* * * * *

In Balladry is many a dream
that the heart hopeless haunts
and one is of the wished for child[16]
love in its loving wants.

And there as everywhere will love
hear only as it would,
wilfully what could never please
heard and misunderstood.

They stood in the dim forest glade,
all had been said before,
she knew that never could she give
what he asked evermore.

'Have I not plighted troth, my dear
with word, yes and with ring?'
'And for that plighted troth, my dear,
my heart will ever sing.'

'I have loved you these many times,
more than are forest trees,
and every time that we were one
wished what love most would please.

What of our so wished child,' he asked,
'the child that you should bear?
Then woman is most beautiful,
as the full moon so fair.

It seems as if some evil blight
came on our loves amain
just like the seed in springtime sown
that never came to grain.'

'My womb, my womb, my childless womb,
it hurts when you are nigh,

many's the child it's born to you
    and every one a sigh!

Oh there was love, my dearest dear,
    your lips were on my breast,
big with all joy my love was then,
    big and so greatly blest.'

'What is it you would say, my sweet,
    our love it has been blest
and all the wishes of my heart
    granted upon your breast?

Say but this once you bore our child,
    secret it bore and still.'
'Love comes in many ways, my love,
    and love will have his will.'

'And what name did you give our child
    that still and secret came?'
'What else but what it was, my love,
    I called it Love by name.'

'And where now is it gone, my dear,
    Love to your breast soft laid?'
'It hid within my heart, my love,
    where it has ever stayed.'

'Tell me no tales, our Love is gone,
    its range the forest wide.'
'Wider than forest or than sky
    yet never from my side.'

'I saw it in the woods,' he cried,
    'run and it ran so wild.'
'That was the wind,' she said and sighed,
    'it never was our child.'

'But I could hear it laugh so loud
    into the sun's bright face.'
'That was the sun itself,' she said,
    'and it shines every place.'

'You did not see it in the stream
    fall and rise up to play.'

'That was the water from the stone
    that fell and went its way.'

He looked into her sad sweet face
    and truth was there to see,
he bent his head to her soft neck
    and they wept silently.

'Love, my love's love,' he said to her,
    'mother and sweetheart dear,
I was a fool to seek the child
    looks from your eyes so clear.'

★ ★ ★ ★ ★

Some moments still on Balladry
    the poet's thoughts run on,
he hears men moving from the wood,
    with them their true loves gone.

Their world is dead, so sad, so bright,
    bright as that scarlet cloak,
sad as the night that saw one love
    take the seventh brother's stroke,

before so glad. Yes, a dead world,
    and yet life never fails,
just as it should be, was it not
    pity that told the tales?

The tears of things, not ours to keep,
    still they will come, go free,
better to share that dead world's griefs
    than self-encased to be.

The land of Balladry sc green
    is withered, wasted now,
leaves sad or bright that rustled there
    are fallen from each bough.

Only a lonely spirit stalks
    under the boughs so bare
and ghostly voices sing to it
    sad songs, none else sound there.

For him no more than Lovers Lane
    the land of Balladry,
once he lived there but that was when
    he loved and so did she.

★★★★★

Notes:

1 This, in sections, uses Scots ballad style, has introduction, treatments of known ballads, ballads of the author, envoi.

2 Such Lanes are still found.

3 Where the brave earl of Douglas is buried in 'The Battle of Otterbourne'. Gold was a symbol of life.

4 To wear such a skirt means virgin love given.

5 The ballads linked here are 'Clerk Saunders', 'Sweet William's Ghost'. A Cypriot version makes the seven brothers come from death as guardians and avengers. Ghosts, as in **Hamlet**, were corporeal.

6 See 'The Douglas Tragedy'. The brothers here may be seven but are not ghostly. What is supernatural is the twining roses. Such twining is in many literatures, e.g. Greek, the Irish `Diarmid and Grainne', and see my tale 'The Geisha'.

7 This is the author's tale, using the device of evasive answers as in 'Edward, Edward'.

8 Deer have been seen to do this.

9 This setting, happily used, is in 'Rose the Red and White Lily'.

10 Green as the colour of extra-marital sex is also in William Dunbar's **Twa Mariit Wemen and the Wedo**, Burns's 'Green grow the rashes O', etc.

11 Methods used to capture Thomas the Rhymer, Tam Lyn, Hynd Etin's bride.

12 Thomas is forbidden to speak.

13 A reference to the great ballad 'Tam Lyn'.

14 In 'Tam Lyn' Janet casts her green mantle over the naked Tam, that is, has intercourse with him and so makes him her man.

15 This tale is an invention and uses no ballad. The hawthorn was one of the sacred trees.

16 This tale, like the three previous ones, is the author's.

OLD AND NEW ORPHEUS

Old Orpheus rode through the night,[1]
    sickness sat sore on him,
vague memories and dreams there came,
    voices and pictures dim,
and now he stood in a dark place
    and felt light round him brim,

sensed more than saw, so slight, so slow,
    the lessening of gloom,
and yet light grew and a faint shape
    seemed on the dark to loom.
Flowers he had plucked were in his hand,
    he could not say for whom.

His horse, no sooner riderless
    into the night was gone.
Not like it. Where, why, was he come?
    These questions on and on
they went and for an answer had
    a dawning, not a dawn.

Something about a need so great
    it drove him from his bed,
made him rise up and dress and mount,
    was loud in his tired head,
but what the words with sound so loud[2]
    were he could not have said.

He spoke and answered him a voice
    he felt he should have known,
and as he listened the years fled,
    he was a young man grown,
his sickness gone. Through a bright wood
    he walked, and not alone,

for with him a young woman went,
    her face as in a pool
winds trouble so not clearly seen,
    through light and shade most cool,
till when they sat he played a tune
    with love of life so full:

love of blue skies and of tall trees,
    the grass so green, air sweet,
the drift of deer, the sweep of birds,
    all life both still and fleet,
but most of love that gives its smile
    to all life it may meet.

So sweetly played that sounds about
    of wind upon the lawn
or leaf that fluttered to the ground
    left off. The last light shone
as his harp ceased, wild flowers he plucked
    for her, and all was gone,

and the first darkness cloaked him round,
    his years now not a few.
Something there was that he had lost
    fresh as on flower the dew,
and from the dark came the same voice
    almost he felt he knew.

'A garland to the courts of night,
    flowers to the sunless hall,
who brings to lay on the dark dais
    where emptiness is all,
whose is the careful plaint that must
    on silent spaces fall?'

Why with these questions was there come
    knowledge of all his state,
memory of companioned hours
    once thought his happy fate,
the coming of the queen of hell,[3]
    loss early felt and late?

She had gone out a May morning
    and felt the serpent's sting,
and the green company was there
    swift as might bird on wing
to bear her under dark green hill,
    her final journeying.

Far, far the hill, a life away
    as he had found it was,

and sadly, sadly come again
    and for too human cause,
he had to look before earth-light
    and for that look his loss.

And now acceptance spoke: 'I seek
    no more Eurydice,
out of this darkness I would bring
    no lost felicity,
but lay these lonely flowers to say
    love was my history.

I shall not knock again against
    the unrelenting gates,
I who have bound myself a fool
    twice over to the Fates
to mock my weakness. I shall sing
    as one whom nothing waits.

No more to walk the high knife-edge
    above the rivered land,[4]
weary and torn from Thorny Moor
    to make the harsh wheel stand
of human pain, and enter hell
    all for a woman's hand.

I shall not play again to Dys[5]
    on harp so movingly
or evermore turn back to look
    on lost Eurydice,
tricked by the love that sought from death's
    sure hand to win her free.

And yet I sing, for in this song
    is a divining rod
to strike the desert of my heart
    and make the stream flow broad,
yes, in the dark halls of my heart
    comes light from the sad god.

Another underworld I know,
    the deep springs of my heart
and no dim shadows come from there
    but blood from every part,

there is the vale though which I go
    and there song's rivers start.

Orpheus will not move again
    or beast or bird or stone
and if he plays a tune that's sad
    he plays to one alone,
to the true poet that he is
    that keeps his soul his own.'

'Old man, it has been often said,
    "words lie but deeds speak true".
What was the call that brought you here,
    what was the need that drew
you ailing from your bed this night?
    What is there here for you?'

'Darkness that has a shape, I too
    would know why I am come.
Old men have dreams and wanderings
    and my thoughts all and some
forever turn to these sad flowers
    that speak and still are dumb.

But who are you that talk to me
    as if a voice should rise
from winter's earth with prophecies
    of Spring and April skies
and someone walking through the fields
    my heart should recognise?

Why is this darkness lessening,
    why does my heart make choice
to stay or flee and will not say
    what cause comes to rejoice?
Oh ravished shape of loveliness
    too long denied a voice!'

'Orpheus, look at me again,
    am I not fairer grown,
are not my eyes, my hair, more bright
    than ever you have known?
Will you not recognise me now,
    Eurydice your own?'

'Love, is it you again that come?
    Heart, shut these wilful eyes.
Have I not made an end of this
    and learned that all life dies?
Never again, I swore, would Love
    deceive me with his lies.'

'Where else should you have come, my love,
    on this your ending day,
for I have waited long, my love,
    to walk the greenwood gay?
Is Love not beautiful, my love,
    and once come he will stay?'

'Eurydice I have been dead
    these many years for you,
I have been coming a long way,
    only, I never knew,
my every step had the one end
    and Love would have his due.'

'And so will Death, a little while
    and fail will those old eyes,
all sense, all motion, will be gone,
    a body still that lies
on the green earth among its flowers,
    a woman here that cries

for a sick king that rode through night
    to keep appointment gone,
appointment both with Love and Death,
    who saw a light that shone
to show him his beloved, light
    that proved but a false dawn.'

'No, no, my love, nothing was false,
    Death opened kind a door
to let me see you as I do,
    this once and nevermore.
He comes, but I rode well this night
    to see you as before.'

'Gone is the old King Orpheus,
    by men and ladies loved,

who patient stayed his horse and heard
    their plaints, by pity moved,
who put aside his own great griefs
    as kingly him behooved.

Glad am I, glad, my old love came
    on this his ending day,
was never any end for him
    but the one wished for way,
grown old in love that still for him
    meant his Eurydice.

I could not say this was no end,
    for his old body yes,
I showed him I was changed, he saw
    only past happiness,
still I was the Eurydice
    of youth's fond memories.

Death set a seal upon my lips,
    but he is dead and now
rises from him new Orpheus,[6]
    the life Death must allow.
I wait, he comes, my love as bright
    as blossom on the bough.

Orpheus, look at these young hands
    and think what they must mean.
Are they not the same hands that played
    so sweetly to our queen
and almost won me from Death's will
    to what our loves had been?

Those old man's clothes, old flesh, you wore,
    all so unfittingly,
were not for the new day, they went
    with all past wear to be.
As our own selves we now stand up,
    of all encumbrance free.'

'I knew an end. You speak of selves
    fresh as on their first day.
What of the pains and pleasures I
    gathered along life's way?
Is that poor body, all it learned,
    to pass from memory?

And why was I not told?' 'If such
a knowledge should come in,
how would men act and feel? Would not
the world all new begin?
No, not from the outside comes good
but from the man within.

Nothing is lost, the things that were
live on, he lives in you.
But I have waited long, my love.
They loved as spirits do,
so much more one. Too sudden change
his newmade being knew.

'I wanted you too much,' she said.
'To me as much unknown
I did not think what love entire,
two souls to one full grown,
could mean. And such things wait
as none should meet alone.

It was for this I asked to come,
our queen could understand
how you would be in the first days
stranger in a strange land,
and need the love that once was yours
for guide and still at hand.

Death's entrance may seem one lone point,
its land is limitless,
never will we see all of it,
enough for a poor guess.
It is in that so far green hill
to judgment they process.

There souls come kind are met with smiles,
others admonishment,
kept strait until their better selves
show, then forgiveness sent,
and so made free to love their kind
as always had been meant.

No queen of hell but death our queen,
she knows the heart's demands

so of her grace she let me come,
    wait in these wooded lands.
I watched her as the strings you swept
    weep for those moving hands.

When she must come she comes, but then
    pities each hapless fate,
and most a lover's. Did she not
    plead against Death's set date?
Yet you could feel they knew your heart
    never would let you wait!

And for a look there I was lost,
    love's look, untimely, made
a broken compact. Self-undone
    you went, your lost love stayed,
all for a look made desolate,
    left a still widowed shade.'

'Eurydice, your queen swift come
    and you torn from my sight
it was as if life's day had lost
    the best part of its light,
and on my spirit fallen was
    only one lonely night,

as if I now haunted a house,
    its one dear presence gone
and empty, empty, every room,
    no face to smile upon.
I heard your voice in the still night
    and missed it with the dawn.

For you I would go wandering
    sad in the greenwood gay,
I played, the very beasts would come
    and mourn in sympathy.
At last the journey perilous
    along the hopeless way,

and treacherous. Courage came least
    of all strengths in demand.
More than knife bridge the siren songs
    from plenty's rivered land[7]

near brought me to a stumbling death,
    drowned in the rich flood spanned.

And more than simple thorns sharp set
    this body had to meet,
the fearsome way of Thorny Moor
    pleasured with stings most sweet.
I had to dull all senses there
    or stay for thorns to eat.

And over all of Thorny Moor
    it seemed a song was sung
that was of flesh. With every sting
    I saw your serpent's tongue.
It does not matter now, my love,
    May with its blossoms sprung

is month of passions and you met
    a man. I nothing said,
it was not you that took his love,
    desire the season bred.
Not only you that morning died,
    your lover soon was dead,

a friend of mine. Remorse so preyed
    on both you could not live,
and I, love given, found I had
    love just as great to give,
though sadder now.' 'Occasion made
    a love quite fugitive,

and yours I knew was not. To Death
    I took a tarnished name,
my love for you felt no less great.
    A good man shared my shame.
Forgiveness I would ask the day
    into our land you came,

one cause why I so grieved when you
    both won and lost me there.'
'You make me glad, I knew our hearts
    had too much love to share
for one lapse to make any less.
    Green never was your wear,[8]

Let me go on. One act alone
pleases in afterthought,
three felons vengeance put to pain,[9]
I did not ask for what,
mercy's few strains upon my harp
released and on I sought.'

'Yes you won through, and I was proud
as you came in the hall,
as bright as any spirit there
you fought and knew no fall,
the sadder I when at the last
one moment spent it all.'

'And do you wonder? When I won
and turned back to Earthgate
so very, very far it seemed,
uncertain still our fate,
soundless your step, I had to look
and know my fault too late.'

They stood, the two, hidden in light
and looked back down the years.
'Do spirits ever cry?' he asked.
'I was a thing of tears,
the harp that had moved others made
no music to my ears.'

'Orpheus I knew well your pain
for a lost happiness,
out of the darkness of your mind
I drew those images,
the sunless hall, the courts of night,
yet flowers there nonetheless.'

'It needs no saying,' he replied,
'yet this once it is said,
"I love you". Look, the dawn comes up,
see that bright tinge of red,
so still dawn, day and night, come round
and the sun's dance is led.

His partner is the hidden moon
and as he wheels away

she takes his place, in constant dance
    returning night and day.
So will not be our dance, my dear,
    close partners we will stay'.

He looked down at the fallen man:
    'I should not be so sad
for that once young, late failing form,
    in it I made you glad,
it knew delight in its own kind,
    beauty as nature bade.

After the labours, sports of day
    sometimes pursued with zest,
it would go home to evening peace
    and kindness on your breast,
even in age with all its ills
    it knew the sweets of rest.

No, I should not be sad but am,
    loss never left old eyes,
it took me walks, with me would tire
    of sun and summer skies,
with me could wish when morning came
    never with sun to rise.

My house of life dream-haunted was
    and, love's dream found, it died.
No better ending, yet,' he stopped
    and on a thought he sighed,
'its rooms imagined running feet,
    voices that called and cried.'

'All that is done with now,' she said,
    'vain wishes, pain and play,
it does not help, it does not help,
    remembering his day!'
'Yet pity comes,' and they looked down
    and handed turned away.

His people found him in the wood,
    wild flowers lay garlanded,
whatever pain had come to him
    from that still face was fled,

what the dead king did in that place
    none of them could have said.

Yet one there was that thought to hear
    distant a music made
passing away, and as it went,
    before it came to fade,
by woman's voice accompanied
    a harp unearthly played.

★ ★ ★ ★ ★

Notes:

1 There seems to have been no poem on Orpheus' death, an old Orpheus or my 'new Orpheus'.

2 On my wife's death I heard her voice ring loudly through my house, had to get up and look, the voice too loud for words to be heard.

3 See Robert Henryson's **Orpheus and Erudices** c. 1480 for the queen and journey imagery. In this poem hell is replaced by a bright realm of death, but to Old Orpheus it is dark hell. Henryson took the green hill of the Fairy Queen as in ballad and legend, its inner world was bright.

4 See Henryson and later notes on this imagery.

5 Dys, another name for Pluto, god of the underworld.

6 The new Orpheus and his new world are the main change in this poem.

7 As in Henryson, there has always been an anti-capitalist strain in the Christian tradition.

8 Green was the colour of wanton sex.

9 Ixion's wheel has been mentioned, the other two are Tantalus the greedy, Titius who wished to know too much.

TROILUS AND CRESSEID[1]

1 Farewell

Cresseid went to the Greeks,
toy in a ten years war-game.
'Look after yourself,' he said,
"Look after yourself for me"
was his meaning, and those about
could not know of that other place
where his arms held beauty
perfect so that it hurt.
'Look after yourself,' said then
were words from such pain of longing
and wish she were held again
to hurt with as perfect beauty.
Cresseid went to the Greeks
and out of his life, not love.
It was the best of wars
the old men said, fought for a woman,
something hearts understood,
as his did then.

2 Meeting

One foolish battle more and known for such,
time for siesta both in tent and town,
pavilioned Greeks and men in chambered Troy,
among these Troilus, though his bitter war
less for Achaians than a woman lost,
now as he thought in Diomede's Greek arms,
or cast-off and a common prostitute.
And yet he loved, and empty arms desired
as once with Cresseid he had known desire,
still one might find the other, still might sleep
quiet, content, in their good world possessed.
    But that imagination could not last,
the gentlest missives all unanswered went.
He wrote upbraiding, though his pain spoke most:
'I could say "Go to hell",
and you would go and I would be in hell,
and so nothing is said and this is hell.
Hell is charactered by long silences.

We are all hypocrites in hell,
none choose to come but having come
all choose to stay. Hell has a face of love
for each of all its loveless citizens.'
Troilus heard the rumours of the day
but lived still in the nights of Cresseid's love.
    So on a day folly turned back to Troy,
life's chances unconsidered, all his thought
on self betrayed, and where he sadly rode
a company of beggars hemmed him round,
the best to see disfigured, hideous,
the blasted tree sending its pale arms wide.
'Alms for the living dead' was all their cry.
One woman in proud silence sat apart
in her unseeing grief.
Troilus meeting Cresseid by the way
did not remember her,
a mask of many loves was on her face
as any woman's these days that he saw.
Her skin had the white tinge of leprosy
and yet he thought on Cresseid of Troy town.
Some sentimental coin stayed at her feet.
She wondered at this strange benevolence
and her proud spirit wept.
Troilus learned, one of the living dead
and then just dead. A woman's arms
all that made sense of life, he sought his end.

★ ★ ★ ★ ★

Notes:

1 For 1 and 2 see end of Chaucer's pathetic **Troilus and Crisseyde** and, mainly, Robert Henryson's tragic masterpiece **The Testament of Cresseid**.

NAISI WITH DEIRDRE[1]

'Deirdre, long promised queen
    to Conachar, oh hear
my last remembering
    now that his step draws near,

not of our meeting eyes,
    nor flight to Alba's shore,
but of our first of nights,
    my darkness in your door,

and eyes upon your bed
    where moonlight let me see
your beauty wait, and how
    it seemed and was to me:

as if an old and simple
    world once again began
where you were just my woman
    and I was just your man,

and in our house of loving
    we lay down side by side
and the night made you, Deirdre,
    the too brief night my bride.

I sigh, I sigh, my Deirdre,
    for the first house we had,
it was in green Glen Etive,
    the living there how glad!

Dreams we had then, my loved one,
    of children you would bear,
the lifting to the breast,
    the lips that fastened there.'

'Such dreams were mine, beloved,
    even before that night.
I dreamt in heathered Alba
    the days of long delight.

Why did we come back Naisi,
    not to hear death's close drum

beat out your last hours, minutes?
    Naisi, why did we come?'[2]

'I came for simple reasons,
    once more to see my land,
and I was told in childhood
    a king's word had to stand.

We came on a king's promise,
    holy my father said,
if not, from earth, the living,
    all truth and trust were dead.'

'And so we came to Erin,
    though my true heart misgave,
the ambush of false Erin
    and your untimely grave.

Would we had stayed in Alba,
    your haunt the hills so free,
and known the peace of evening,
    the peat fire kind to see!

And yet I cannot think it,
    surely the gods must spare
the fine flower of your life,
    let pass the cutting share.

Life owes us happiness
    or why should we have met?
And certain in Glen Etive
    in full it paid its debt.

I will not hear that trampling
    of horse about these walls!
Still I am back in Alba,
    your voice homecoming calls.

Say it is true, my Naisi,
    happiness is the rule,
the days filled with a brightness,
    the nights so beautiful.'

'It is not like that sweetheart,
    the years, they bend and bow

and slow but sure they kill us,
    it might as well be now,

now when that old world entered
    is but as yesterday
and all good things it meant, love,
    are live in memory.

Think only this, this only,
    what Conachar will mean
we know, but he will win
    only a mocking queen.'

In the beleaguered house
    the son of Usnach spoke
with Deirdre, knowing Death
    not long withheld his stroke,

and soon he must go out
    and battle hopelessly,
as he had loved, and no
    more his beloved see.

And Deirdre holding him
    saw run a road before[2]
and a rock rush at her
    and she saw nothing more.

Notes:

1 Deirdre (Diredree) was reared to be queen of Ulster's king, but fled with Naisi (here = Nysee) son of Usnach to a glen by Loch Etive in Scotland then Pictland, called Alba by incoming Celts. Lured back to Erin, Ireland, by promises, he was killed, She threw herself from Conachar's chariot, her brains dashed out on a rock.

2 Deirdre had vainly protested against the return.

THE BARD

Summer and evening and the village tree,
how many bards before him had it heard,
had one said what he was to say that night?
The folk were settling to their listening,
but it was to the young that he would speak,
had he the words to reach them, make them hear?
Soon blind, his eyes still saw the nearest and
his smile embraced them, in them lived the hope,
already they belonged to times not his
and his bard's spirit strongly moved in him,
he felt the presence of the yet unborn.
When would the change come? It could come in them,
inheritors not of a past but life
to come. The vision, **that** had made him bard,
not the mere memory that others had,
the ancestors, their deeds, how small a theme,
their sayings - but the folk were silent now.
'Children, you know this was a land of giants,
great stones they set on stones, roads, bridges, built,
things not of stone that you must wonder at,
and then made light of their own handiwork,
left it to time's unmaking, went away.
Where no one knows, not the most learned bard,
the ages keep a silence, how or why,
though some have thought the endless open sea,
tempted them, wearied with the narrow view
our fields afford, and sought another land;
others in the far north where mountains ring
their secret valleys place their settlements,
but the few travellers returned tell tales
of a waste land, themselves sicken and die.
I think the sea appealed, a greatness there
of their own kind, or the bright-scattered sky
to their winged spirits, for some carven walls
show great things built and pointing to the stars,
such craft and cunning in their restless hands.
Was there a war that shattered all their works?
But who would dare? Among themselves you ask?
A question all too ready to our minds.
I cannot think it, makers as they were
would they unmake their own, except to do
some greater better thing? No, wise as great,

they went is all we know.
    Why should you heed
an old man's thought? And yet I like to think
one day without word spoken they could feel
their homeland call, and with the next were gone.
Home is where all would be, unknown as known.
Why do I say this, we are little men
but with great feelings, and our daily fields
for hours can look quite strange, a looming hill,
even some skiey point, can speak to us.
It is as if we knew this was not home.
Children, I see you and I ask myself
how long till the call come and you too go.
And now I say a strange thing, when you go
forget the work of giant hands, designs.
Perhaps this in the end is what they knew,
their homeland, like your own, was not in things.
Man needs his house, his clothes, his food, the means
to be himself, express himself, past these
is what you see around, a waste, his life
is all within and there his greatness lies.
Go children when you can and find that land.'
    The bard ceased, had they heard him, understood?
The folk were gone. No, some way off a boy,
a girl, looked long at him. He felt tears come.
The boy nodded, he did not see them go.

★ ★ ★ ★ ★

WINGS

A name that to this day for me
has a sad magic and, all said,
will have it still for what it means,
is Icarus, young Icarus.
No craft that ventures into space
dares use it, and no man that hears
the tale of flight and fall but he
reflects upon his life and thinks
to each his own Icarian sea.
    Young I have said, he was so young,
his heart too readily airborne.
No stop expected in his flight
he sped as joy speeds home to joy,

as the rapt soul pursues its prayer,
the Cretan boy whose melting wings[1]
lost him the freedom of the skies,
and his life too, as unforeseen.
When first the dreadful change began
he never knew, no warning felt.
The sun seemed brighter, warmer too,
so kind a smile on that great face
as if for him and welcoming.
So swift the ending came, there was
only a shock of blank surprise,
a moment's childish wondering
and foolish in that lonely sky
he felt the winds snatch either wing,
the heavens refuse him utterly.
He fell and falling once he cried
to Zeus whose purpose never swerves
from chosen paths, and so he died.
The waves, like him in rise and fall
bore up his name as still they do,
'Lost Icarus! Lost Icarus!'
seabirds and sea together cry.

A fable meant for man, not boy,
not of flight failed but hopes denied,
of other heavens that refused
their too brief visitor his joy.
Yes I can see a boy that lay
idle on seagirt heights outstretched,
admiring how white wings would fleet
in such a confluence of grace
as none could watch and not once feel
a wish like powers to possess,
out from the cliffs to see them soar
sunward unhesitant a joy.
But children, young men, they are more
practical than their elders are,
I see the boy rise up, forget,
and go among his day concerns
as if the vision never was,
life so immediate for them,
its present asking everything.

Much more it is the man I see
go thinking on known happiness,
the bird that in life's room had flown

and stayed as it would always stay,
then in an instant ever gone,
so to love's thought it had to seem
days that had wings but kept no height,
out of the sun so suddenly,
the moment of love's object lost,
perhaps that once a cry enforced
past the vain purchase of a prayer,
then the descent to whelming waves
of overcoming loneliness;
after, the sobering of days,
thinking at last more patiently,
life but exacted its strict due
that he should love it and love there.

Notes:

1 In the Greek fable the wings had waxen fittings.

SHORTER LOVE POEMS

WINTER'S DREAM

You ask me about daffodils
    and is their season here.
No daffodils bloom in the Park
    for Spring comes late this year,

but I can dream another scene,
    sad Nature at its best,
Nature that is so bare these days
    in you so brightly dressed.

No daffodils, yet I can dream
    black hair a golden shade.
Oh I will dream you anything
    that Nature can parade!

In you shall all the seasons be
    but summer most of all,
the great sun rise and fall in you,
    bright days be at your call.

So the best season I will dream,
    always the best for you,
love like an early morning's walk,
    fresh on the flower the dew.

What does it matter if the dream
    be only dream, no more?
The day I cease to dream will be
    the shutting of the door

on life and love. Soon will come Spring,
    your golden heads at last,
winter well gone, but we will dream,
    love, it will not have passed.

NOW

They speak of man's eternal being
under a happier, brighter sky,
but I am now and ever have been
and ever will be till I die.

For now is when my arms go round you,
now is my thousandth fond embrace
when I still seeing you am moved,
still see as the first time your face.

And so it is through all day's stages,
now is a place where time stands still,
as on the bridge the looking lovers[1]
signal their souls and ever will.

Now in her orient is my love,
and she is fair and passing fair,
I think of gardens and of flowers
and she the fairest of them there

now dawn is come. Oh you my love
fill all the stations of my sun
in his bright passage of the sky
first in your orient begun.

Now is when noontide is at highest,
the sun near strips the park of shade
and yet we find it and our loving
in its kind shadows there is made.

And now is when beside the river
we lie and kissing is no game,
and my lips find your lips forever
one moment with your whispered name.

Now is the afternoon about us,
you answering me sigh for sigh,
and now is the late light that tells us
soon to the day to say goodbye.

Now is the sunset seen as smiling
on day and all days gone before,
as we on love and all our loving
now that for us is evermore.

★ ★ ★ ★ ★

The clock is ever in my thought,
    it will not stop,

second by second round the day
    the hand is brought,
and midnight still is you
    as day thereafter.
What should make it stop? Not you.
    This mechanism
owes nothing to your care, or mine,
    it goes quite punctually
and it is past repair.
    There was a moment when
I felt it start, and endlessly,
    and that was when we met.

★ ★ ★ ★ ★

Notes:

1 Reference to the Willow Pattern.

THE PARK

When you put on your summer dress
    how much you mean to me!
I think as to the park we pass
    you are the loveliest She.
But soon as in my arms you come
    beauty is not enough,
you are no more my summer girl
    but everything I love.

When you unscarf your sunbright hair
    hands gentle as are eyes
reach wondering for its thousand lights
    as children do fire flies,
but in the moment we embrace
    my feelings are quite blind,
and in the eclipse our kisses make
    it's you alone I find.

And after, handed as we go
    upon a grass so green

and by a river calm and clear
    like none was ever seen,
it seems, as swans go queening by,
    white ships with white sails furled,
and round them busy cygnets ply,
    for you was made this world.

I dream, no more we walk that world,
    no summer comes to show
what song is in the heart to sing,
    what sunshine there can flow,
vanished the park, the pair that looked
    into the river clear,
who could imagine grass so green
    and happiness so near.

Youth is remembered into age
    just as if yesterday,
you are and are not the same girl
    who walked that summer way,
but I can dream time kept you there
    lone figure in love's haunts,
and that you hear me now and know
    all that my heart still wants.

My lips are lonely for your lips,
    my hand to touch your hand,
and walk beside you, my dear love,
    into that other land.
You are that other land, my dear,
    that I will never know,
and if I walk beside you now
    it is in dreams I go.

★ ★ ★ ★ ★

THE FLUTE

Were I a flute held in your hands,
your lips to touch my every stop,
what music would you bring from me,
what airs to make my sad world dance
and ease its heart of love upon!

Or were you flute, the player I,
how happy should my fingers be
to fetch a pleasure from each part
and waken sense to ecstasy,
so the rare instrument I played

sang with the life that in it cried.
Then, then, perhaps as silence fell,
clasped in my still remembering hands
still should I dream that rise and fall,
still waken to as sweet unrest,

and play again; so intertwined
player and played should be as one,
not selves but one pure harmony
of an enjoying perfect soul
that to another world is swept.

So youth could play but kindly age
and quiet presence had their tune,
the evening's room was full of it,
I listened and when you left off
I cried to hear again its sound.

And now an idle flutist wants
his flute and sighs that it is gone
with all the music it contained,
all stops untouched, all tunes unheard
that late so sweetly thence were drawn.

And yet he dreams, dreams it is here,
and lifted to him tenderly
meets his lips as it met before,
so playing is shared happiness
and blissful past or tune or word.

Dreaming he holds it as he held
it once when soul upon it sang
and his sad earth was made a heaven.
Now in its silence he can hear
love's perfect voice and only that,

not the known voice that late he heard.
The flutist loiters without flute

in park, in lane, on bridge, alone,
and the flute playing in his mind
is lost in long remembering.

* * * * *

JOURNEY

My soul has gone a journey infinite
even upon the instance of your kiss
and come again to do the same again,
such distance I have travelled on your lips.
Nor have my hands stayed still, unmoved on you,
stroking your woman's softness they have seemed
to touch the utmost mark of tenderness,
the deep-down kindness that is loving flesh,
and that too was a far-sent travelling,
so I went dreaming on your lavished breasts.
And if flesh set me on such journeying
what shall I say of eyes your windowed soul?
Only that from these my own soul looks out,
calls and I go. Dearest, the infinite
is yours to give, yet love asks limits too,
as of a room, your quiet company
making that resting-place we call our home.
Again, not travelling as senses may,
nor quiet from such travelling and still,
but on good earth to walk and feel the sun,
so we were handed, of our loves assured,
that were enough, then near and far all one.

* * * * *

FAREWELL ON A STATION PLATFORM

It should have been in a green park
and in some shady green retreat,
I should have held you in my arms,
both done so many lovely things,
suffered no one of love's alarms
as passing voice, approaching feet,

and in that long close afternoon
loved as the sun went down the sky.
Yes, that is how it should have been.
Then would have been a time and place
to say all the occasion meant.
But in an all too public place,
a station crowded, there we talked
and to the minutes of the hour
said hurried, pointless things, if I
am right, just once 'I love you'. And,
what had the gun strapped to my side
to do with love? People about,
but we embraced, the whistle went.
Strange that tight feeling in the breast
as if for love quite wholly lost
when only for some five years left.
That said, a station platform
was no scene for so great a death.

* * * * *

DAFFODIL

Golden heads atop green dresses,
bodied slim as youth should be,
Nature is the best dressmaker,
knows the season and its wear,
swaying in their crowded parties
through the woods on holiday.
I can hear the old trees talking,
'Were we young and fresh as they?'
So I see those lovely ladies
men call golden daffodils,
how the winds their sudden lovers
bow them, bend them to their wills.
Comes a calm, the daffodils
stately stand untouched and free
as no lovers there had been.
Why do I see you among them,
not gold-headed nor green dressed,
swaying to the winds in beauty
and when still, still beautiful?

I can see you so wherever
life and loveliness may be.

* * * * *

THE SUN-STARVED CITY

Spring kind and cruel to lovers
comes to the sun-starved city,
mixes the bran of blood,
laughs as the pale ghosts flock.
I with them turn to my sun,
feel through these lust-cold veins
the course and sting of desire,
flinch from the expected laughter,
age is absurd. And yet,
are we not much more than lovers?
Human, do we not hurt
and hurting turn to each other?
Something that might be pity
stirs in our close embrace,
something that knows about living
and comforts itself with a kiss.

* * * * *

GIRL FORSAKEN

Once there was a time
the blue bird would hover,
waters happy run,
I was with my lover.

It was Spring and leaves
danced so wild and free,
flowers laughed at my feet,
he picked one for me.

Than I seemed his joy
and I was his love,
what he asked I gave,
could not give enough.

Time was I would walk
glad his arm was round me.
When Grief came at last
in love's field he found me.

Now no more together
and of love forsaken
still I feel my hand
into his hand taken.

Yes, I lost a lover
with no love to give,
weeks I wandered lone
with no will to live.

Yet I ask the future,
if he happened by
would this passing stranger
take me with a sigh?

★ ★ ★ ★ ★

THE FOOL

It was inevitable, Time came too,
came with us all that wretched afternoon.
We had known him be such marvellous entertainment,
that day he was a dreary dull buffoon.
We laughed, he was so ludicrously sad,
taking the whole thing much too seriously.
We chatted brightly, but his stubborn gloom
damped our best efforts till we three just sat
looking as if the end of things had come.
All through the park and on the seat he'd gloomed
as if from the one thought he could not stray,
and when at last we saw you to your train
and said goodbye he stood so very still
I thought the fool would never move again.

★ ★ ★ ★ ★

REFRAIN

Some time I have been listening
to the clock ticking on above

the spreading quiet of the room,
and playing with such images
as should beget a peacefulness.
And now such quiet comes as if
just out of hearing a small stream
talked with itself, its one clear sound
the still repeating of a name
heard as the burden of a song,
the song that you have made my life.
Like a bare foot the old refrain
plashes the waters and they speak
of love at last come to its peace.

★ ★ ★ ★ ★

How have we known the robes of fire
about our burning bodies fold
and the mixed metal of desire
been for an hour all purest gold!

How have we lain before the sun
and seen the high tides leave the land
and from the shore white horses run
and the sea settle warm and bland!

How have our loving bodies said
such fond farewells, while on the bay
westered the sun in gold and red
and splendour left the dying day!

★ ★ ★ ★ ★

POSTCARD

A legend from our fabled past come live,
insisting that it happened, once was real,
the colours that had faded with the years
suddenly bright again. Why did you send
out of your silence and so long lapsed love
this painted scene? Had that one yesterday
of all our yesterdays stayed fresh in mind
and spoken from a card to memory?
A man, a woman, stride an upward slope[1]

leaning into the effort of their climb,
the packs they carry speak of far intent.
The grass stands strangely spiked, small flowers upright,
upon a bough a bird sits timelessly,
there is a stream, a bright line of descent,
and in the distance mountains blue, snow-capped.
The painter does not aim at photograph,
yet life is stilled, the more intense for that.
They will toil on forever, side by side,
and a foot never move, enchanted pair.
You saw in it our day's continuance?
A scene unreal, yet it can touch me so
our vanished world a moment shows again.
When was it we last dreamt, so long ago
and in the picture entered of our dream?
Nothing there real, but real things bettered there,
as beauty made more beautiful by love,
and light on all things all ways that we went
not borrowed of the sun. Oh we dreamt well
in those ideal days, as never since,
and now a postcard makes relive our scene,
the loved, the everlost. So let us go
and by the way of many little flowers,
the touching of the hands, the brief caress,
that all proceed of love's great gentleness,
seek out the country for a moment was.
A day, what is it to our changeful lives
more than a moment years may dispossess?
Some things are changed, the painter sought effect,
to stay time's flow, vainly to fix our scene
that even as we lived it had to move.
Then the green blade would bend before the wind
that now stands straight, leaves from their trees would sing,
the bird sits still upon its too bright bough
that startled should have flown. It was a world
of movement we strode through, of things that lived
and therefore had to die as that day did,
but if that movement's gone the dream's the same.
We do not talk, peace is on all we see
and quiet with our mood the stream flows on,
the still expression stolen on its face
is happiness, two walkers in the sun
as we were then. Ahead and clear to see
are the blue mountains our sun shone upon,

perhaps too blue as if those sharp peaks rose
out of an ever gentle land below
and kept the nature of their origin.
    How wise the painter was to hold that scene,
lay down his brush, not let his subjects climb,
though he could not have known as we have known
what must have happened then, the change to come,
irrevocably lost the dream. They ward
that other world, the legendary life
with its sad fables: one about a pair
that went and never found their way back, still
wandering in the foothills and despaired,
an echo of their voices seeming borne
to the high passes and there heard as real,
real as a hurt child's cry than which nothing,
nothing's more real. But that has no place here,
here in this painted picture of a dream.
Why should a legend live to hurt again?
Lucky for me I stumbled upon life
that let me dream as never legend did.

★ ★ ★ ★ ★

Note:

1 I should be grateful for an identification of the painting that once suggested this poem.

THE ROSE AND THE NIGHT WIND

In vain the dance by changing music led,
in vain remembered what each change had said,
the end to which it danced said all it meant.
Above the red rose grieving the wind leant,
so lately on its stem by passion tossed
beauty upon the night air had been lost,
and all his doing. There was ecstasy,
tender her giving and so kind and free
when he had taken her, leaf after leaf.
And now he was alone and with his grief.
It did not help that she enjoying died
and with the last leaf had no more than sighed.
Nothing for tears, nothing but fond regret
for that sweet more she might have given yet
the red rose felt, not so her lover wild
that with her end could not be reconciled.
All night he had made love to his red rose,
taken no thought for beauty, how it goes,
only he saw and sadly saw near morn
beauty was lost, of all its leaves quite shorn,
and mourned his love, her latest perfumed breath
so haunting him he chose the sleep of death.
Who can believe at first the loved one dead?
Where she lay now love too would make its bed,
so slept the wind and rose together, still,
at one in death as had been the wind's will.
Night's dew fell on them where they stirless dwelt
and in its falling was no longer felt.
Music was heard on the still air to rise
and fall, descend to where dead beauty lies,
ascend in triumph for what beauty gave,
a love that did not stint and did not save,
no less for the fond lover in his end
and all such selfless loves time yet will send.
There comes another wind, another rose,
sadness and yet a triumph in the close.
Into the storm-rent garden blows the dawn.
One watcher with head bowed, the music gone,
still dreams that perfect finish in pure pain,
not all his love can fill the stage again,
nor all his dreams design the dance anew,
the dancers fled and from the rose the dew.

Sightless he rises, goes where his feet will,
beauty that's dead dancing before him still.

* * * * *

THE TWO DREAMS

The full white sail sweeps on,
its speed made clear by the one passing cloud.
How long since it cast off to be alone?
How strange the night without remembering moon!
Pay him no heed, my loved one, sleep your sleep,
nor once look up there to remember me
for whom you were a dream within a dream,
whose arms dreamt round you, lips on your lips dreamt,
who waking cried to dream again, sleep on.
    Sleep while I go with him, the wanderer,
that in lone watches of the vacant night
wonders that earth so soon should lose its loves.
Where are they when the night and he return?
So brief love's interval and bravely spent
before the dark, not that his light dispels.
New loves but bring the saddest brightening.
And yet he sails, still seeks the port of dreams.
Before him should be huge discouragement,
but all he sees his harboured rest at end
and loss made good. Great dreamer of the night!
Meanwhile relief is in his memory
and in its lighted scenes. He sees you there
in youthtime beautiful, and dreams on you,
the girl you were who meant so much to me.
    Forgive the moon, the too intrusive moon,
that under night a thief enters your room,
steals to your bed on silent silver feet
and stands to take the spoils of memory
for comfort on his lonely voyaging:
there the still face beneath dark pillowed head,
eyes closed in sweet containment like a flower,
the quiet rhythm kept of easeful breasts,
but to his fond gaze sadly undisclosed
the limbs that late had moved in loveliness,
last and not least the smile on parted lips
that half remember love and lover's kiss.

All this the moonlight dreaming on you shows,
all night he lies with you till with the dawn
warned by its coloured sounds he rouses, flees,
kindness that's beauty's best the day must see.
Was it such years ago and seems but now?
Still through the Garden, Park, and to the bridge
above dark pool that sends no image back
of your felt beauty hand in hand we walk
and your full smile grows ever more my sun
till all smiles cease upon a given kiss,
an impulse of impossible pure love.
Oh we had walked elsewhere and loved elsewhere,
but had not felt such bond as we felt then.
And when a day came never out of mind
the bond stayed fast that was to seeming loosed,
absence was found not such a final thing,
passage between the two worlds was resumed
and simply came with closing of the eyes,
not that so happy union of earth-souls,
but union still. I dreamt, at first refused
what brought no peace, then almost peace I found.
I had a dream, the foolishest fond dream
was ever dreamt by mortal under moon
in his lone hour, happy, unhappy, dreamt.
And still it haunts me. Could it come again?
Far, in a distant kingdom, sleeps my love
and bits and pieces of her earth sojourn
visit her, pass, remote, indifferent;
dreams come and go, scenes from that other place
unstayed, dismissed the most as meaningless,
not touching her, for what should touch her here,
though two child voices sometimes will intrude
and then she knows her residence of loss.
Else substanceless these mists of memory
forever shifting past, mere dreams indeed.
Yet one there is that comes most hauntingly,
there was a man she loved in that far world
and dreaming lips remember if not feel
the kindness of a kiss. The day was bright,
they stood upon a bridge, the wanting arms
went round her as most wonderful and dear
of all things made. Yes, once she had been loved.
Youth was upon them, it was kissing time
and it stayed with them when love's fullness came,

youth's scene it is that now she longs to live.
    And as she dreams she knows that he too dreams,
and the same dream, the two dreams can be one.
She stirs, she goes, she stands at his bedside,
he in his dream opens his arms to her,
she enters and once more it is as when
they stood upon the bridge and arms went round.
And if one kiss was real so too is this
since both of love. Unfelt now his embrace
as was the moon's when he came visiting,
unfelt her love yet still by him returned,
her presence known as in dream-sight it is,
the stroke of love on her no less unfelt
and yet dream hands still moving a delight.
That they made love is a dear memory
so his desire once known fond arms receive,
she lives in dream all joy on earth she knew
and after shares with him its given peace.
How had joy grown a stranger and so long?
And now a sadness finds their dreaming bed,
day has to come, he wakes, the two dreams flee,
yet nothing of their night but goes with her
and on his lips, last scene of young love dreamt,
lingers her parting kiss.
    It asks a price to step out of one's self
into the world of dream. Where I had been
past thought so happy by so much the more
I was made desolate
for vanished beauty not to come again.
But if it could, if it could come again,
if but an hour, if but one little hour,
'Then that full sail in heaven might enter port
night's voyager no more,'
mocks the plain sense of things, another voice
more gentle seems to say, 'The way is known.'

* * * * *

'I think you are completely beautiful.'
My hands were wondering at your sunbright hair,
so much to learn and you were all my school
as if I'd never studied anywhere.

Lips never taught so much as yours did then,
the fierce blind understanding of a kiss

made you all women and myself all men,
you were completely beautiful, my bliss.

Yet all we said said nothing, how we said
was all our meaning, eyes that love was kind
and lips that it had made us less alone.
Entered on life the now no more undead
with the exploring fingers of the blind
found beauty that till then they'd never known.

* * * * *

HOME

This garden I have made,
this home is made by you,
it will seem one day here
best happiness we knew.

In his cot sleeps our child
who played at such a pace,
he will wake with the sun,
laugh into its bright face.

Still you are busying
yourself with household things,
it seems to me our house
with quiet purpose sings.

Look with what easy fires
the summer heaven burns,
how bland the day suspires,
how clear the night returns.

If it were always thus,
to feel such evening grace
settle so deep in us,
making one quiet place,

if our desires at last
stayed and put off to roam,
if into day night passed
and still we were at home!

* * * * *

The woman and the dream
    always together
come, as now it would seem
    they come in you,

for it is womanly,
    has breasts of love
and they bend over me,
    grace beyond touch,

infinite beauty shown
    in a fair woman,
the way time best makes known
    its dreaming soul.

The smile that lights your face
    there is the dream,
kindness its moving grace
    and beautiful.

Kindness is all, it says,
    and without that
the hope, it vanishes
    of child, of race.

Haunts me that quiet smile
    into the night,
and day, a dreaming while
    that does not fade.

* * * * *

LOVE AND CHANGE

Everything we love
    changes and passes,
like a spirit goes,
    wind in the grasses.

Love is such a child,
    tell its oft-told story
any different way
    it will miss the glory.

As my love is now
    I must always know her,
as the morning sun
    rises still to show her.

Thus, if she should die
    and be changed that day
bitterly I should think
    she is gone away.

If her earth-fled ghost
    sought me glorified,
loving, yet I'd say,
    'She indeed has died.'

HELEN

You are as beautiful as my own thought,
for it is you that make it beautiful,
it is for me a calm and shining pool
where your fair face these many years I've sought.

You are as beautiful as my own soul,
souls are for giving and you give so much,
all I can mean is that I learned some touch
of kindness from your smile and not the whole.

Thought, soul, if they have beauty, it is yours,
how could I learn the whole, who had no call,
you suffer and yet look beyond it all,
you smile the kindest smile, and nothing cures.

And in the end it is your smile endures.
I reach out for your hand, it reassures.

★ ★ ★ ★ ★

Why should I fear when time's small stealth
will deal us ordinary doles
of love, who had in it such wealth?
Why? In remembrance is my trust,
that makes best moments live again.
Still will two lovers mount the slope

and on the heights their hearts remain,
lost ever to that dim low land,
where never they will go again.
There on new heaven's brink, my dear,
they will remember, do as when
lovers newmade they stopped and kissed.

★ ★ ★ ★ ★

SOMETHING INCOMMUNICABLE

At the world's other end you sleep -
for so it is, so far from me
in this bright hell of desert sands -
your beauty made a still machine
the coin of light must operate
to play the music of your smile.
Such lovely sound when I saw you
I had to listen. Here and now
the still wind-driven sands of death
blow hourly. With man's little help
death does its work efficiently.
A brilliant but exhausted scene,
loud colours but their music faint,
the sun sets all to the one tune,
the moon bright-rising does the same,
a variation in their sound
has briefest life. That rare thing rain
coursing the wahdis of the night
is lost and squandered in the plains,
silenced its roll of drums. At best
these are the desert's sound effects -
let us forget the angry guns:
dawn comes a clash of cymbals, and
night trails a fading winding horn
after the sunset's violins,
they make no music, and still heard
stale the ear waiting something new,
only a killing sameness here.
    Think how it was. The usual day
in all its stages had a song
that gave the time its loveliness,
and came from you. I hear it yet,

all other sounds that sight may bring
are ordinary sounds to me.
What saves my soul along these sands
is the still haunting of an air
out of the past come beautiful
to spell me with the theme it sings,
the smile upon the face of life
you gave to it, that will not go,
'Listen,' said Vasudeva, 'to[1]
things incommunicable that
are felt and never can be told.'
Such is my saving love for you.
Your speaking look an unheard voice
still seen, it ever comes with me.
I listen and it does not cease,
still it sounds on, as does your smile
heard singing continents away.

★ ★ ★ ★ ★

Note:

1 See Hermann Hesse's novel 'Saddartha'.

IN OUR GARDEN

The garden burns and broods sun-hazed,
its burnished paths and beds bloom-rife
glow out of time, each flower seems phased
in an illusion of still life,

as if such stillness meant to say,
'Our business only is to be
and yours by coloured paths to stray
lost in the loveliness you see.'

Now windless dream the daffodils,
they do not wake to sigh and sway,
watcher and watched on one still stream
are borne from life and time away.

The appleblossom faintly gleams,

the crocus burning from the lawn
a pure spiritual flame now seems
the gazer stands to dream upon.

Yet nothing in all this spells out
as symbol for eternity,
something indeed it talks about,
how brief our season has to be.

I see how things grow to an end,
beauty is best before it dies,
our thoughts touch in their sunset trend
beauties, not truths, of paradise.

Dreams there may come we call divine,
feelings above the earth we own
seem like a witness and a sign
of something more than beauty shown,

but that is now enough for me.
Within the garden I can sense
the burden of the mystery
and know it, though in innocence.

Helen walked here, I walked with Helen,
its pool of beauty stirred and broke
and was the smile I know as Helen,
it was as if the garden woke

and life in tree and grass and flower
was felt for all their moveless peace,
they had lain spelled in summer's power,
she smiled and life had its release.

★ ★ ★ ★ ★

PICTURE

As every other night he wakes,
looks on the face so much he loves
and his mind other pictures takes,
and love's old mood within him moves,

moves the fond gazer as he sees
imaged his dream of womanhood
under the blossom-haunted trees
and smiling out of quietude

to miss the live original.
Beauty, he thinks, has but one style
and it is love, he can recall
the passing of that lovely smile

under the pressure of his lips,
how at such moments day was night
and underwent such kind eclipse,
sad for the soon return of light.

Oh those were kissing days, blue skies,
and he a lover and in bliss,
life was the promise in love's eyes
and that fulfilled what could he miss?

Yes, love was beauty's only style,
such understanding of life shown,
in the slow dawning of her smile
a tenderness near pity known.

Of course she wore his given ring
that sealed her to him as his wife.
Yes it was there, his love began
quiet into the night to sing
the song of woman and her man
loving few days, than loves for life.

★ ★ ★ ★ ★

IN REMEMBRANCE OF HELEN

(1) Hour of Grace

It came quite suddenly and all unsought
as best hours do,
I was alone, too much alone,
I thought of you:[1]
and quiet with the morning I was come

not to awake you from much needed sleep,
meeting with so great silence in your room,
seeing half open the unseeing eyes,
finding belief in death so hard a thing
where love has been.
Expected, but the moment never is.
You lay forever so.
Yes, certain things would now be done,
but that is what my days will ever see.
    Since when so much unreal, an empty house,
the presence missed from it that made it live,
the centre lost, and in its taken place
life's mere continuance, so much you meant.
I set a table, no one smiles across.
One thing, the days of my unreason, they
are gone, the vain protest, lost all control
the angry and exclamatory times,
there is a reconciling and it came
upon the hour of my relieving grace.
As I began, thinking back to your death,
so I went on, I went remembering,
but now your life, and this made easier
by giving it the distance of a dream
as more and more it seems.
    You led me handed to a gentle land
lovely and strange, yet one so well I knew
having so often looked into your face
and seen it there. It might have been the east
so bright it shone, you its unsetting sun,
a sun I felt would always stay noonhigh,
I never thought upon its westering.
The day saw me go out, saw me come in,
I had not left for still I was at home
with you there waiting and our two loved sons.
Love-longing, love fulfilled, that land might know
but most your peace,
and such content none after comes like it.
Fancy indeed might have thought that it heard
great wings still passing, passing, overhead,
the bird, the wings, of love.
    Oh clouds could come and night most heavy fall,
there was a loss,
my sudden burst of tears your arms contained.
And yet bright days resumed their visiting

as you would have them do,
not vanished but receded to the shades,
withdrew before your sun that still would rise
the worst of griefs. So through that land that wore
the face and features of a dream, and yet
so suddenly could change, changeless you led.
    Led through that land despite infirmities.
Hardly you let them show at entering,
yet even then the intervals of pain
and seizing ache were frequent, and with the
downbearing years expected company.
What will was yours to live as others do,
how much unfit! Still you endeavoured till
in a taxed body a heart overstrained
gave final warning, sadly understood,
you would not see your loved grandchildren grow.
Gone now the gentle land, save in a smile
though kind now ever sad. It had been you
that kept it still in being. With you went
the features of the dream, they were your own.
    My hour was gone that was your gift of grace,
evening was come and sad into my room,
along the street the cherryblossom snowed
as if late Spring took on a winter's tinge.
You had not left me but all that bright east
where you had led me from your face was ceased,
only the great wings passing still were heard
as they would always be.
And yet things sad I now saw new,
that so still face upon the morning's bed
was beautiful as no face I had seen
for the remembered love.
Those eyes late closed, they had closed well on life,
for now it came to me,
acceptance they had worn and with a smile
on your last night. It was the only wear,
and still to smile was more than to accept,
it meant a day well won.

Note:

1 My wife Helen died 4 April 1989.

* * * * *

(2) THE GREAT MUSIC

When the great music sounds, sound hill and glen,[1]
street and green park, men know the piper's tune,
but with it the more ancient silenced song
that is their country's, and some moments are
themselves again.

As now in evening's park the pibroch cries
and cries and folk leave talking, in their ears
loud the ancestral voice, a storied voice
that stills all others, a sound rising on
the haunted air.

And I that come here only for the listening,
listening and seeing seeming almost one,[2]
I let the rising sound be all of me,
too soon it goes and leaves me to myself,
a songless thing,

songless as I have been since you fell silent,
tuneless this life you left, and yet, and yet,
out of the past your face, is it not music
that I can see and hear, and waits on me
to sing its song.

Songless I said? The sound is all about me
as of an ancient song still new and sung,
the pipes lament but now for all dead lovers,
dead but so that their stories have lived on,
their music heard,

sad voices, vain unanswered questioning.
Where now is Deirdre who with Naisi fled[3]
and come again in Erin made an end,
and where is Grainne for whom Diarmid died,[4]
life's water spilled?

They walk upon the nightwinds, with their song
now woven is your own, of love and sad,
the pipes they cry it as they cry all other
songs for those living, loving, to brave end,
life, love denied.

For if brave spirit ever met its ending
as it had lived, then surely it was yours,
hidden the fears, forced that last night your smiling,
with morning it seemed to me that you slept,
Helen, my love.

Pibrochs, they wail for stricken battlefields
and may not love be such a stricken field
where slain or wounded lovers hapless lie,
their spirits crying for what once has been
and is no more.

Grief, still the heart may hear above the keening
tones of a triumph for the love that was,
for the true loss is in the never knowing,
the never giving, these the saddest souls
and most to mourn.

Play piper, play, play quiet for the dying,
stately and measured for the loved one dead.
Such griefs in loving! Cry from the battlefield
dead love's brave beauty, how it made an end
and lost and won.

Now are the pipes made silent, but remembered
is the great music that you made for me,
yet it plays on, though now you do not hear it,
and will play on when I am silenced too
in this your song.

Notes:

1 Pibroch, pipe tunes often, not always, martial, with variations, are sometimes so called.
2 The piper's kilt belongs to the tradition of his music.
3 See my 'Naisi with Deirdre' (Diredrie).
4 Grainne (Granyie) with Diarmid fled her old husband Finn. As Diarmid lay dying Finn thrice fetched the healing water of life and thrice let it spill from his hands.

* * * * *

(3)

You paid your visit, came and went,
    you will not come again.

My life is a blank paper now,
    mine is an idle pen.
Who would have thought such boundless space
    between us two could lie!
There was a bird flew in my room,
    flew out to its far sky.

* * * * *

(4) SUNSET

The sun is dying,[1]
great fires flare and burn,
its red and golden splendours
tomorrow will return.

In our lives are evenings
that give us pain
for red and golden suns that set
and do not come again.

* * * * *

Notes:

1 Adapted from lines in Ruben Dario's **Cançion Otoñal**.

OTHER THINGS

SEAGULL

Beauty like a crying gull
    is swept across my skies,
through shifting clouds a fleeting face
    from banished paradise.

She wheels before the frowning brow
    of rock that fronts the sea
as if one hour it should grow clear
    life God's forgivingly,

as if it were that high fierce hedge
    round Eden tenantless
and her soft breast eternally
    against its thorns must press.

Always her lost distressful cry
    sounds like a separate soul
that neither claims the solid earth
    nor seas beneath that roll.

At times I watch her beat the cliff
    with impotent shrill wings
as if she fought there desperate
    the cold grey heart of things.

And I have seen out of calm seas
    cruel storms like great cats spring
and leaping moan and hiss and spit
    beneath her blooded wing,

and the great rock from which she fell
    and beat upon in vain
watch like a Pharoah carved in stone
    the spectacle of pain.

★ ★ ★ ★ ★

COMMITTEE MEETING

The chairman of the meeting doodled on, as he had always done, thought Michael, and

such clever doodles too, like time and space,
though what to do with them he could not see,
restrictive was the word that came to mind,
and matter that defined them, was it real?
Of all the supernumerary hells
his was the most, thought Lucifer, boredom
like a strong rain that never would leave off.
Hell was his own invented word for it,
forever running errands to and fro
for someone else, none for himself. Heaven
was no democracy, a concept come
aeons ago upon the dullest job.
With 'Other Business', the last item on
the day's agenda, he would make his plea,
speak up for private judgement, choice, free will.
Of course, already his mind had been read,
as he read Michael's, not the Doodler's, and
that was not fair. What did **he** have to hide?
Michael was frowning, a true army man
though he had never fought a war. Orders
were orders, patient aeons he had sat
his mind at the salute, prepared for what?
He was quite sure that Michael did not know.
The Doodler was quite different, he seemed
to view him as a source of contrary
and therefore useful thoughts, but would he take
this one on board? He looked on space, there should
be something, someone, there to interest.
'Sometimes you can be quite original,'
the chairman said, and his pen moved once more.
And now he had stopped doodling. They could see
two naked bipeds standing by a pool
and smiling so their image smiled again.
'Adam and Eve,' the chairman briskly said,
'and the expression on their faces love,
a new idea.' Lucifer sat up
and looked respect, for beauty, hope, were here,
a will. Almost he missed what next was said,
'Your business is to wipe away that smile.'
Lucifer thought, 'Defect!' 'That too,' said God.

* * * * *

Along my way a child
smiles to me, I

wonder how if life smiled
    always like that?

It does not, yet it must,
    else the wind howls
over a desert's dust
    despairingly.

'Nothing discovered can[1]
    be undiscovered.'
That it found wasteful man
    the planet sighs.

Notes:

1 An argument of Margaret Thatcher for the retention of nuclear weapons.

★ ★ ★ ★ ★

CAFE

The people come and go,
wait the too well imagined woe,
they leave their cars to drink
where the heart need never think
and talk and laughter keep
them feverishly asleep.
I sit here where the town goes by
and know its will,
that dreams should hold it till it die,
the dreamer's heart then still,
and I reflect
on folly vainly circumspect.

★ ★ ★ ★ ★

A TEEMING WORLD

Dinosaur days, flick of the lizard's tail,[1]
high pterodactyl scream to small bird's song,
aeons, such aeons in a nine months womb

quickened by meeting with one lover's sperm,
life runs so strong.

Where are the great beasts gone? Climatic change
that after many million years betrayed
their appetites? Were they so stupid that
they outbred life and stripped their planet bare
for lusts unstayed?

And the new king of beasts, so much more bright,
intelligent, that from his soul aspires
so splendidly? It seems he too outbreeds
his means, and still a crowded world and waste
teems and desires.

There are these sayings, 'He that runs may read',
'The hungry generations tread us down',
'We are betrayed by what is false within'.
In the old comedy romance was played
a white-faced clown.

Dinosaur days, flick of the lizard's tail,
high pterodactyl's scream to small bird's song,
aeons between, no such momentous change
as a race instinct towards self-control.
Could I be wrong?

Such seems the history life re-enacts
and without dignity, the simple doom
and tragedy of lust: voracious wombs,
the too, too many voices, one mad cry,
'Make room, make room!'

And all this said, nature no less protests
your right to breed the wished-for child in you,
to know the beauty of love's tenderness
above the baby lifted to your breast,
only your due.

Notes:

1 The descent of small forms from large and the failure of food have both been argued.

* * * * *

THE MEANS

So innocent of man was that blue sky
save for the one lone engine's droning flight,
men out at sea could wonder where and why
it journeyed in that empty world and bright;

its goal Hiroshima, its dormant load
a bomb yet guiltless cradled in its nest
till it was sent, but now so quiet stowed
it did not menace, merely was at rest,

till a touch loosed it and it went its way.
Everyone knows what was to happen then,
and later some would claim that awful day
marked the beginning of the end for men.

The means control us, as an idle boy
sees stone and bird and knows the killer's joy.

* * * * *

One world I would not wish to know,
where change of man's estate comes slow,
one where the pastures of the mind
offer no joy to the wild foal
but the great cattle wander blind,
content, not singular of soul.

* * * * *

PURITY[1]

They look at the same life, so what they see
is error, these like-seeers, and they breed
from their one vision evil that breeds death.
Nature is diverse in its human loves
and faiths and truths, and so creates,
but they seek the one virtue purity,
and that destroys, with kindred consequence
of cruelty, for mere humanity

gets no respect from them, quite meaningless
its counsel to be kind. Purity kills.

★ ★ ★ ★ ★

Notes:

1 From a personal statement of the Japanese novelist Ibuse.

LINES

'At the great forest's boding edge
the pool immovably expects
its vital issue, long aware
where in the light and shade involved
the snake of centuries proceeds,
is shaken to be ever still.'
So the words wrote themselves unwilled,
but to my merely passive mind
only a forest lived and night
sibilant by the usual pool.

★ ★ ★ ★ ★

FANTASY FOR A FIELD-BURIED SOLDIER

His eyes are all the brighter
now that they flame as lilies,
his body lies the lighter
now that it lies as earth,
the winds shout perfumed music
from many kinds of trumpet,
from his corrupted body
now comes the season's mirth.
I wonder if the soul
the priest had prized so much
snuffs on the winds of spirit
a breath so pure, or such
as where this chymic body
makes gold of coarser clay
and gives to careless children
violets and pinks for play.

For him no withered tributes
but flowers that live and grow.

* * * * *

Time passed on,[1]
time went its way,
happiness a leaf
on a river lay.

Afternoon is waning,
already it dislimns,
after it a cloud
like a vessel skims.

Vessels of the heavens
make to your goals,
on to the impossible
carry our souls.

Vessels of the heavens
go save our dreams
where in empty heavens
hope most lonely seems.

* * * * *

Note:

1 A version of Arturo Capdevila's 'El tiempo pasò'.

SPINNING TOP

The boy intent
on the for him deserted walk
plays his lone cosmic game,
moves and is moved, a god,
frees his wound string,
himself fast bound and spelled considering
the spinning of his top.
It falters, fails, indifferent he goes,
released from his own spell by a lapsed world.

One day a world will stop
that moved with all his feeling and his thought
and leave him not indifferent.

★ ★ ★ ★ ★

For most life's too insistent sore
is ordinary with the day
as if it were an order given
and their small souls must still obey.

No such long habit could be yours,
you had the unconsenting will,
you chose and you went quite alone
where all your human hurt is still.

★ ★ ★ ★ ★

It is no petty course this world,
here the aspiring runners race,
like a flag suddenly unfurled
they pass the many-headed face.

These are the Achilles' who should win,
Ministers, magnates, commissars,
the tortoise is our ancient sin
and has the betting of the stars.

★ ★ ★ ★ ★

JERUSALEM

'Do you see it now?' asked Richard,[1]
and the knights standing by him on the hill
said, 'We can see Jerusalem.'
'Is it not beautiful? Does it not shine
like God's own angels?' 'Yes,' they replied,
but none could look that way
for watching where the young king knelt, back turned,
hands pressed in prayer and his wet eyes
seeing in the dull glitter of the sands
the city of his faith, his failure too.

'Is it not beautiful?' he asked again
and heard then answer as before.
Not one of them had seen Jerusalem
unless it were the king, and they in him.

* * * * *

Note:

1 A Spanish legend makes Richard as penitence for failure to take Jerusalem deny himself the sight of it.

ABERDEEN CHARTER

A day set, business in the Chanonry,[1]
charters to be made out, confirmed, revoked,
the tenantry of a Scots diocese
compearing to its summons, a day kept.
'The plea of David Brown,' the archdeacon said,
'who now resigns Corchrony, dues unpaid
for hardship of the times, making request
that a more able cousin wield the land.'
'The plea is heard,' the bishop said, went on:
'We know how Adam his goodfather fought
at Falkirk and at Wallace' side and died,
there something more than a mere thrifty man,
for freedom of this kynrik and its kirk.
We too have dues we cannot pay, at least
we can remember them. Let Adam's death
be entered in the charter with our grant.'
This was in thirteen hundred sixty eight,
the bishop Alexander Kinmount and
for his archdeacon John who made the *Bruce*.
Charter and verse are shelved now, freedom too,
for thrifty men know nothing of such dues.

Note:

1 A 'day set' was an appointment in a court. Other Scots legal terms are 'compearing', 'heard', used of a plea for 'granted'. The Chanonry is that of St Machar's Cathedral, Old Aberdeen; the charter is now with the University Library. The archdeacon is John Barbour patriot and father of Scots poetry, his **Bruce** 1376-78. In the last line the contemptuous phrase 'thrifty men' is from Hary's epic **Wallace** c. 1478 where it is used in the same way.